SHAKEN NOT STIRRED

SHAKEN NOT STIRRED

A CELEBRATION
OF THE MARTINI

ANISTATIA R MILLER & JARED M. BROWN

HarperPerennial
A Division of HarperCollins*Publishers*

Excerpts from *Autobiography* by Noël Coward © 1986 Estate of Noël Coward, reprinted courtesy of Reed Books. Excerpt from *Ian Fleming* by Andrew Lycett © 1995 Andrew Lycett, reprinted courtesy of Weidenfeld & Nicholson/The Orion Publishing Group, Ltd. Excerpts appearing on pp. 23, 94-95, © 1996 Shaken Not Stirred™, reprinted from the 1996 Shaken Not Stirred Martini Story Competition (www.martinis.com/key/contest1.html). "The Morroccan Odyssey," © 1996 Gerald Posner; "Fishing Story," © 1996 Corren Larson; "Mr. Extra-dry," © 1996 Chris Madison; "Smoked Martini," © 1996 Steve Starr. Excerpts from an interview with Marc Nowak on pp. 57-58, 81, and 85, © 1996 Shaken Not Stirred™, reprinted from the Seattle Martini Competition (www.martinis.com/key/X0020.html). The Muscovy, Alexander Nevski, and Mikhail's Martini recipes, © Carillon Importers, Ltd. reprinted courtesy of Carillon Importers, Ltd.; Oliver's Classic, Fortunella, Royal Wedding, Sterling Gold, L'Orangerie, Mandarin Martini, Peppertini, and French Kiss recipes © Mayflower Park Hotel, reprinted courtesy of Mayflower Park Hotel; Becco's, Banana, Red Skyy, Tatouni, and Merchant's James Bond recipes reprinted courtesy of The Alden Group; Berlin Station Chief, Golden Triangle Station Chief, and Paraguay Station Chief © Jeff Carlisle and Charles Wharton, reprinted courtesy of the authors; Palace Apple Skyy recipe reprinted courtesy of Palace Kitchen; Spicy Hamilton recipe reprinted courtesy of Sean Hamilton; and La Dolce Vita (Italian Martini) reprinted courtesy of Holger Faulhammer.

PICTURE CREDITS: p. 8, "The Perfect Martini" © Guy Buffett; p. 28, © Mike Peters / Tribune Media Services; p. 79, © Johnny Hart / Creative Syndicate; p. 47 reprinted courtesy of Franklin D. Roosevelt Library; pp. 65 and 119 © Carillon Importers, Ltd.; p. 72 © Bacardi-Martini, U.S.A.; p. 103 reprinted courtesy of NBC, Inc.; pp. 14, 128, and 131 © J.M. Brown; pp. 23, 26, 37-39, 40-41, 43, 50, 57, 108, and 114 from *"Life Magazine" Cuts & Illustrations: 1923-1935* © Dover Publications; pp. 49, 52, and 75 from *Ready-to-Use Naughty French Spot Illustrations* © Dover Publications; p. 31 from *The Great Giant Swipe File* © Hart Publishing Co.; p. 84 from *Food & Drink* © Dover Publications; pp. 87 and 89 from *1,001 Advertising Cuts from the Twenties and Thirties* © Dover Publications.

The term "Shaken, Not Stirred®" is a registered trademark owned by Anistatia R. Miller and Jared M. Brown.

HarperCollins books may be purchased for educational, business, or sales promotional use. For information, please write to: Special Markets Department, HarperCollins Publishers, Inc., 10 East 53rd Street, New York, New York 10022.

FIRST EDITION

Designed by Anistatia R Miller and Jared M. Brown

Library of Congress Cataloging-in-Publication Data

Miller, Anistatia.
    Shaken not stirred: a celebration of the martini / Anistatia R Miller & Jared M. Brown
    p. cm.
Includes bibliographical references and index.
ISBN 0-06-273488-1

1. Martinis. 1. Brown, Jared, 1964– . II. Title.
TX951.M45 1997
641.8'74—dc21

                                      97-2496
                                         CIP

01 ❖/RRD 20 19 18 17 16 15 14 13

CONTENTS

THE MARTINI MENU

(Note: For a Key to the Icons used throughout the text, see page 19.)

CLASSIC GIN MARTINIS

Algonquin 51
Arnaud 41
Astoria 48
Bennett 45
Berlin Station Chief 59
Blenton 48
Boomerang 52
Bronx 50
Bronx Express 50
Chorus Lady 50
Classic American Dry Martini 51
Clover Club 37
Clover Club No. 1 37
Clover Leaf 37
Crest o' the Wave 48
Dean Martini 54
Deano 54
Dempsey 39
Dirty Gibson 36
Dirty Martini 46
Double Tradition 58
Empire Martini 55
Fallen Angel 44
Fancy Gin Cocktail 33
Flying Dutchman 49
Gibson 36
Gin-and-French 29
Gin-and-It 29
Gin Cocktail 33
Gloom Raiser 38
Golden Triangle Station Chief 59
Gun Club Bronx 50
Harry Johnson's Martini 33
H.P.W. 35
Hudson River 45
Hong Kong Special 45
J.P.A. Martini's Martini 30
J.P.A. Martini's Verboten 31
Knickerbocker 34
Lone Tree 50
Martini di Arma di Taggia's
    Martini 34
Martinez 32
Medium Martini 52
Merry Widow 49

Miller 59
Monkey's Gland 39
Montgomery 52
Murphy 36
Naked Martini 53
Old Army 35
Orange Blossom 90
Pall Mall 52
Paisley 59
Paraguay Station Chief 59
Perfect Hatfield Martini 56
Perfect Martini 52
Pink Gin 29
Polo Mallet 48
Princeton 42, 45
Racquet Club 35
Rolls Royce 41
Sidecar 37
Silver Bullet 59
Social Martini 58
Smoked Martini 83
Star 40, 41
Sweet Martini 49
Tightrope 54
V for Victory 53
Virgin Martini 60
White Lady 37
Will Rogers 50
Yale 45
Yellow Rattler 39
Yokohama 39

CLASSIC VODKA MARTINIS

Argentine-Arctic Kick 77
Boston Bullet 73
Buckeye 73
Burns on the Rocks 67
Extra-Dry and Slightly Bruised 74
From Russia with Love 69
James Bond Martini 69
Joe Average 70
Lucky Jim 70
Lucky Martini 67
Mariner's Martini 79
Molotov Cocktail 82
Nairn Falls 78

SHAKEN NOT STIRRED

Octopus Martini 79
Oliver's Classic Martini 81
Pasini Express 71
Saketini 74
Seattle 77
Smoked Martini 83
Stelmach Martini 73
. Tatouni 70
Transoceanic 76
Twist 71
Vesper 68
Vesuvio 77

FRUIT MARTINIS

Apple Pie 97
Banana Martini 95
Bar Marmot Cosmopolitan 92
Black Martini 99
Blue Lizard Martini 91
Blue Monday 91
Captain Lambchop 99
Chicago Blue 91
Cosmopolitan 92
Elegant 90
Fortunella 96
Friend of Dorothy 93
Gilligan's Island 100
Glacier Blue 91
Jack Horner 100
Lava Lamp 99
L'Orangerie 90
Lola 88
Lola Granitée 89
Mandarin Martini 90
Martini Navratilova 98
Melon Ball 93
Metropolitan 92
Miami Special 95
Midori Martini 93
Montini 92
Noonday Sun 90
Northwest Sunset 90
Orange Blossom 90
Orange Flower 90
Orange Lava Lamp 99
Orange Magnet 90
Palace Apple Skyy 97
Patricia Delicia 95
Perfect Cosmopolitan 92
Purple Haze 100
Red Skyy 100

Saint-Lô 97
Seabreeze 92
Spider Bite 94
Sunset 92
Tropical Dream 95
William Tell 97

DESSERT MARTINIS

American Beauty 103
Chocolate Blossom 105
Chocolate Kiss 106
Chocolate-Tini 106
Chocotini 104
Double Chocolate 106
Fawlty Flower 103
Ma Chérie 107
Mixed Chocolate/Chocolate Swirl
   106
The 911 104
Percy Dovetonsil 102
Sakuratini 107
Tootsie Roll Martini 105

SPICE & CAJUN MARTINIS

Alaska 113
Bijou 113
Cajun Combustion Engine 115
Cajun Martini 116
Copenhagen 111
Goldfinger 110
Gotham 110
The Inferno 116
Japanese Martini 112
Mansion Martini 116
Miner's Cocktail 116
Moroccan Odyssey 109
Olympic Gold 117
The 180 113
Pepper Spray 116
Peppertini 116
Spicy Hamilton 116
Spicy Rose 111
True North 113
Wake-Up Call 117
Wild Ginger 117

FLAVORED VODKA MARTINIS

Alexander Nevsky 122
Anastasia 123
Becco's Martini 120
Blanche DuBois 121
Bloodhound 124

Reprinted courtesy of Guy Buffet

PREFACE
& ACKNOWLEDGMENTS

Martini lovers that we are, we launched a Web site devoted entirely to Martinis on Halloween night in 1995. A brief history, a few classic recipes, and some lounge recommendations were our sole early offerings. Thanks to thousands of Martini aficionados worldwide (and our own slightly obsessive natures) our site–"Shaken Not Stirred" –grew and grew. Occasionally, we'd get a note from someone looking for a book on our favorite potable, but we hadn't found a modern volume that contained more than a half-dozen recipes. (The restaurant around the corner has twenty-five Martinis on its cocktail menu.)

Still, we didn't give it much thought until an editor at HarperCollins dropped us a note assuring us that there really wasn't a book that encompassed the variety of Martinis our generation clamors for. He convinced us that we should write it. That was just the beginning. We spent hours, days, weeks experimenting in the social chemistry lab, pushing the limits of clear liquids and stemmed glasses, seeking the drink's ancestral origins in far-off lands, and

The Martini…was a drink that helped define a segment of American society…a more worldly, urbane sophisticate who drank in grand gin palaces fitted out with potted ferns, tile floors, brass railings, and paintings of voluptuous nudes.

—John Mariani,
America Eats Out

The perfect Martini can only be followed by another, and another and…

—*Playboy*,
September 1955

sifting through dog-eared volumes of lore.

Now we all know that a classic Dry Martini is made with distilled London dry gin, as little vermouth as possible, an olive or lemon twist garnish, and nothing else. Any traditionalists reading this book have just gotten their money's worth. However, they're welcome to join the rest of us as we read on, and enjoy some (darned) fine variations created over the past hundred years that also deserve to be sipped from a stemmed cocktail glass.

We'd like to propose a few toasts before we begin, to some wonderful people who've inspired us throughout this project and helped us pull all of this material together.

Here's to our agent Lew Grimes who convinced us to try our hand at launching our first Web site, "Shaken Not Stirred." We are always grateful for his support.

Cheers to George A. Fertitta at Margeotes | Fertitta + Partners for his faith and guidance in gathering research material and making some sound suggestions along the way.

A huge round of sincere thanks to Patricia Barroll at Carillon Importers for providing us with tons of background material, art, recipes, lounge recommendations, and an opportunity to experiment with the new line of Stoli® Flavored Vodkas. Thanks also goes to Samara Farber and Doug Kilzer at Kratz & Co. for filling us in on even more details on a few new lounges and product information.

A round of good cheer to Marc Nowak at the Mayflower Park Hotel, Stephanie Ager of Ager & Associates,

Lola of Lola's at Century House, Masahide Kanzaki of Suntory, Doug Varnes at Set 'Em Up Joe, James Kelly at The Four Seasons Restaurant, Ray Foley of *Bartender* magazine, Lisa at the Pacific Palisades' Monterey Grill, and Clarence Cross at the Palace Kitchen for great nights of Martini fun as well as the art and interviews that they also provided.

Our undying gratitude to Alison Ryley and Wayne Furman at the New York Public Library and Debbie Randorf at the New York Historical Society Library for helping us unearth vital bits of information about the Martini's origins.

A salute to Laura Baddish of The Alden Group for supplying us with the winning recipes from the 1996 Broadway's Best competition and Martini & Rossi vermouth art.

A bow to Laurie Inokuma, our "Essential Japanese" translator, for instructing us in the proper way to order a Martini in the Roppongi with either an olive or a twist.

Hats off to Steve Visakay, barware collector extraordinaire, as well as Gerald Posner, Coreen Larson, Bob Tucker, Chris Madison, Steve Starr, Holger Faulhammer, Sean Hamilton, Ernesto Paez, Stefano Pasini, Jeffrey Carlisle and Charles Wharton of The Policy Hut, Jerry Langland, Clarke Trevett, Pete Miller, Sara Lennard, Jim Hall, and the rest of our Web friends who've visited "Shaken Not Stirred."

A rousing toast to our HarperCollins team including our editor and toastmaster Jeremie Ruby-Strauss who found us on the Web and drove us to drink, our

ODE TO MY SIXTH MARTINI
Rising high above
the bar,
Your frosted stem
reveals how chilled
you are.
Clear and crisp
and dry as dust
I'll drink you now.
I will, I must.
Oh perfect gin Martini
No one shall e'er
impeach you.
Now, if only I could
stand upright,
just long enough
to reach you.

publisher Linda Cunningham who believed in the project, Jason Rhodes and Joana Jebsen in marketing who make things happen when the writing's done, our cover designer Joel Avirom who made us thirsty with his vision, Rose Carrano and Karen Schachter in publicity who helped us get the word out, Kate Stark in Retail Sales and Malachy Noone in Special Sales for seeing beyond the bookshelves, and everyone in production and copyediting who had a hand in making this project a real live book.

With that done, there's only one more thing to say: Let's party!

Cheers!

Anistatia R Miller & Jared M. Brown

INTRODUCTION

The Dry Martini is the one true Martini in much the same way that a fine Bordeaux is the only red wine. You'll get about the same results in a restaurant if you simply order a Martini as if you simply request a glass of red–either way, you're at the mercy of the waiter or the bartender. You might end up with a house-brand California varietal table wine or an excellent 1993 Chateau Margaux Pavilon Rouge. With a Martini, you might get a Medium-Dry, an Extra-Dry, or a chilled glass of gin served either straight up or on the rocks.

I always remember my first Martini…by the third one it gets a little fuzzy.

All Martinis have the same basic ancestor–mixologists call them short drinks. (Long drinks are served in tall tumblers and contain an 8:1 ratio of non-alcoholic liquid to booze.) Professional bartending guides categorize Martinis along with their close cousin the Manhattan: a blend of whiskey/scotch and vermouth. So even in the minds of the experts, this particular cocktail branch has a fairly broad range of species and subspecies. Just like any plant, animal, or mineral on earth, you can apply scientific classification to build the Martini's family tree as we have here:

ALCOHOLIC BEVERAGES (SPIRITS)

COCKTAILS — OTHER ∴

LONG DRINKS ∴ — SHORT DRINKS — OTHER ∴

Manhattan — Martini — Daiquiri — Marguerita — Other ∴

Variations (e.g. Rob Roy)

Variations (e.g. frozen banana)

Variations (e.g. frozen strawberry)

Gin Martini
Variations (e.g. Dry Martini, Alaska Gibson, Negroni)

Vodka Martini
Variations (e.g. Cosmopolitan, Lava Lamp Copenhagen, 911, Spider Bite)

A Latin scholar from Cambridge walked into The Mill Pub, took a seat at the bar, and called to the owner, "Give me a Martinus, please."

"You mean Martini, sir?" the owner inquired as he pulled out a fresh shaker.

The scholar hastily answered, "If I want more than one I'll tell you."

Modern Martinis have created an even broader definition for the "king of cocktails." Exactly what definition? You could say that a Martini is a short drink made with either gin or vodka and served straight up in a Martini glass. Concoctions that prescribe cognac, tequila, or whiskey as their main ingredient are definitely not members of the esteemed Martini family.

What about a Martini served "on the rocks"? It's just that: a Martini served on ice cubes–just like a Vodka Martini is *a* Martini, even though it's not *the* Dry Martini. Besides, these narrow parameters are a pretty recent phenomena that developed during the postwar 1940s and 1950s when upper-level executives dictated America's –and the world's–tastes.

We've uncovered over a hundred Martini recipes that were created during the 1920s and 1930s. Variations are not a new trend, they're a rediscovery of worldly individualism.

Finally, we pondered one more serious question that befalls every serious Martini drinker: when's the best time to drink one? In Ernest Hemingway's *Islands in the Stream*, it never seemed to be too early or too late:

It's never too early for a cocktail.

—Noël Coward,
The Vortex

> ...[Thomas Hudson] looked at his watch. "Why don't we just have a quick one?"
>
> "Fine. I could use one." [Roger replied].
>
> "It isn't quite twelve."
>
> "I don't think that makes any difference. You're through working and I'm on vacation. But maybe we better wait until twelve if that's your rule."
>
> "All right."
>
> "I've been keeping that rule, too. It's an awful nuisance some mornings when a drink would make you feel alright."
>
> "Let's break it," Thomas Hudson said. "I get awfully excited when I know I'm going to see them," he explained.
>
> "I know."
>
> "Joe," Roger called. "Bring the shaker and rig for Martinis."
>
> "Yes, sir. I got her rigged now."
>
> "What did you rig so early for? Do you think we're rummies!"
>
> "No sir. Mr. Roger. I figured that was what you were saving that empty stomach for."

MARTINI ZEN
THE ART OF FINE MIXOLOGY

*See, in mixing, the impor-
tant thing is the rhythm.
Always have rhythm in
your shaking. Now a
Manhattan, you shake to
fox trot time; a Bronx
to two-step time. But a
Martini, you always shake
to waltz time.*

—Nick Charles,
The Thin Man

NORA CHARLES:
*How many drinks have
you had?*
NICK CHARLES:
*This will make six
Martinis.*
NORA CHARLES:
*[to the waiter] All right.
Will you bring me five
more Martinis, Leo? Line
them right up here.*

—*The Thin Man*

So you already know how to make a darn good Martini. Frankly, that's not good enough. You want to make the best Martini that ever graced the inner curve of a thoroughly chilled long-stemmed cocktail glass. You don't just want a Perfect Martini (*see page 52*); you want Martini perfection! No? It's your first time, and you just want your date–who's arriving for cocktails in ten minutes–to believe that you've made a Martini before? Either way, read on!

The first thing to realize is that there are very few components to a Martini. There are the ingredients: gin (or vodka), vermouth (or its replacement), garnish, and ice. Then there's the equipment: a cocktail shaker or mixing glass and stirring spoon, long-stemmed glasses, and swizzle sticks or toothpicks. That's it. So it's through the proper manipulation and balance of these few items that you're going to produce liquid satin instead of a drink that'll leave you licking stamps just to get the taste out of your mouth. This, young Grasshopper, is Martini Zen.

FOUR DEADLY SINS
OF MARTINI MAKING AND DRINKING

If you aspire to being a master Martini mixologist there are four things you must avoid as both participant and responsible host–the guardian of your guests' health and happiness:

Deadly Sin No. 1: Use the finest ingredients you can afford. Mixers like soda, tonic, or juice can hide a multitude of sins, especially when they comprise the majority of a drink. But in a Martini, that's not the case. This cocktail depends on the quality of its few ingredients for its flavor. Since most of that is the liquor, if it's no good, neither is the drink.

Deadly Sin No. 2: Drinking games. Save group entertainment for lower-proof drinks like gin-and-tonics or beer. It's like going four-wheeling in a limited-edition Range Rover. Sure, it'd be fun –but what a waste. You may not need a permit to carry one, but a Martini is not a toy.

Deadly Sin No. 3: Using aluminum mixing implements. To quote one visitor to our Web site, "Bleeeeeccchh!" Aluminum degrades quickly when it comes in contact with acids (like lemon oil or juice). When it does, this metal imparts its unique essence into the mix: a liquid version of nibbling the wrapper off a Hershey's Kiss. Likewise, copper and, some say, silver have the same effect. (Although we suspect the latter might just be the tarnish cleaning off into your drink.) Stick to glass or stainless steel implements–the strongest flavor in your drink should be the drink itself.

Deadly Sin No. 4: Performing certain physical activities. Anybody can remind you and your guests not to drink and drive. We completely agree (don't drink and drive), but we'd like to add a few other cautionary notes. Please *don't* drink Martinis and rollerblade; snowboard; ski (either downhill, cross-country, or ski jump); handle unsheathed Samurai swords; play darts blindfolded; walk the tightrope wearing hockey skates; wrestle alligators; gnaw on electrical cords; attempt to re-enact O.J.'s

The last time someone proffered a spirit in a plastic bottle near me, I waited until it was empty, brandished it in front of the cretin –who'd completely forgotten by this time that it wasn't a genuine glass bottle–and discreetly whacked him over the head with it. After he realized he wasn't dead, he spent the rest of the evening over-using the same gag on anyone who'd stand still long enough.

famous low-speed highway chase; swim; complete your federal tax return; play the French horn; walk barefoot on hot coals; monopolize the karaoke microphone; or anything else that goes against your sober common sense.

If you find all this a bit restrictive, you'll be glad to know that there is one activity that requires copious Martini consumption *before you begin*. Take a vacation in the Philippines and join the locals hunting for venomous sea snakes. Before they enter the coral reefs, divers drink up a storm to fortify themselves while they work. According to them, if you have enough alcohol in your bloodstream, it protects you from the sea snake's deadly bite.

A PRIMER ON TERMS AND MEASURES

Until you get used to counting or eyeballing your measurements like a pro, it doesn't hurt to have a shot glass with indications for 1 oz. (30 ml) and 0.5 oz. (15 ml) printed or etched on the side, a teaspoon, and a tablespoon in your bar equipment inventory. There are also a few bar terms you should learn to recognize:

1 dash	=	0.33 teaspoon
1 splash	=	0.25 oz. (7.5 ml)
1 tablespoon (1 T.)	=	0.5 oz. (15 ml)
1 pony	=	1 oz. (30 ml)
1 jigger or shot	=	1.5 oz. (45 ml)
a twist	=	0.25"-0.75" x 1.25"-2.25" strip of lemon peel
light Martini	=	2 oz. Martini
regular (standard) Martini	=	3 oz. Martini
large (boardroom) Martini	=	4 oz. Martini

double (Chicago)		
Martini	=	8 oz. Martini*
Straight up, Up, or		
Chilled neat	=	served without ice
On the rocks	=	served with ice

* Save the toothpick. Use it to dial AA.

POURING LIKE A PRO

Did you ever see the movie *Cocktail*? Yes? Did you go home and make a total mess of your kitchen like the rest of us? Okay, so those shakers were glued shut, the bottles were sealed, and who knows how many retakes they actually did to get those bottle-tossing, drink-flinging scenes right. But the actors couldn't fake those perfect pours. With a little practice, you can pour just as accurately.

First, go buy a couple of those nifty tops they use on liquor bottles in bars. (Most kitchen equipment stores have them. They're called speed pourers.) Go home, fill an empty liquor bottle with water, and stick a speed pourer on it. Grasp the bottle by the neck and turn it completely upside down over a shot glass. Count to four (or five if you prefer) in the time it takes to pour a 1.5 oz. shot. Next, try pouring to the same count into a regular glass. Empty the contents into the shot glass to see how closely you measured. Figure it should take about a hundred pours to master this skill. (That's why you've got to use water.) From there you can easily enhance your repertoire by pouring a splash (a one count), a dash (cover the little opening with your thumb and pour a one count), and a drop (cover the big opening with your thumb and pour a one count).

KEY TO ICONS

Stir. Fill the shaker halfway with ice. Add ingredients, and stir contents for at least 15 seconds. Strain and pour.

Shake. Fill the shaker halfway with ice. Add ingredients, affix lid, and shake for at least 8 seconds or until it's too cold to hold. Strain and pour.

Let stand (aka: an in/out). Fill the shaker halfway with ice. Add ingredients, affix lid, and let mixture stand for at least 15 seconds and up to 3 minutes. Strain and pour.

Garnishes.

Special tips or mixing hints.

Variations.

Toasts.

One argument in favor of stirring versus shaking: Stirring gently produces a much clearer Martini. Shaking adds tiny bits of ice and tiny air bubbles, which tend to cloud the drink.

James Kelly, head bartender at the Four Seasons Restaurant in New York –and one of the world's best mixologists–demonstrated his Martini-making method for us. After filling a glass shaker with gin and vermouth, he then stirred the mixture rapidly for precisely twenty-one seconds. Although he never glanced at his watch, we secretly timed him as he repeated the process for each of three Martinis. Maybe our ability to read our watches slipped a little, but his timing didn't falter by a second.

The first rule of shaking is to make sure the lid's on tight. (Do this every time. Unlike pasta, you can't tell if a Martini's done by tossing it against the wall to see if it sticks.) Then hold the shaker at a slight angle and shake gently with an up-and-down motion. Vigorous shaking throws a lot more ice shards into the mix.

CONTROLLING THE STRENGTH

Other than the obvious (more or less booze), it's easy to make a Martini stronger or more user friendly. Here are a few tips:

- Crushed or cracked ice melts faster than cubes, adding more water to the mix when it's shaken.

- Room-temperature liquor instead of freezer-chilled has the same effect: it melts the ice faster.

- The longer you shake the mix, the more the ice melts.

SHAKEN NOT STIRRED

- Using freezer-chilled vodka or gin and mixing without ice makes a stronger drink, but keep in mind that the right amount of dilution really helps the flavor.

PROTECTING THE FLAVOR

You may have gallons of the best vodka or gin and premium vermouth, but if you haven't touched those freezer-flavored ice trays since you moved into your house, you've ruined your Martini before you've begun. Ask yourself these pertinent questions before pouring those precious liquids over the cubes:

- Did you wash the trays before you made the ice?

- Is the ice fresh? Or is it encrusted with the frosty remnants of last year's chili-fest?

- How's the water? If the tap water you use to make the ice tastes funny, so will the Martini, unless you use bottled water.

- If that doesn't seem to work, a box of baking soda in the freezer might be the cure.

- To really impress or baffle your friends, you can add all sorts of things to the ice (no plastic bugs, please). Some of our favorites are: a dash of vermouth or Cointreau, flower petals, or a splash of cranberry juice cocktail.

THE QUALITY OF THE GARNISH

High-quality olives or a fresh lemon twist are the perfect finish to the per-

HARDWARE

- Cocktail shaker with a tight-fitting lid or a stirring glass and shaker set (glass and metal)

- Cocktail strainer (coil-rimmed)

- Long-handled bar spoon

- Martini (cocktail) glasses

- Bar towels (clean dish towels)

- Cutting board

- Sharp paring knife

- Ice bucket and tongs

- Double-ended metal shot-glass with a jigger (1.5 oz.) on one end and a pony (1 oz.) at the other (or a shotglass with the measures marked on the side)

- Speed pourers (optional)

- Cocktail napkins and toothpicks

After cutting twists, wash the knife immediately. The acid in the lemon dissolves the micro-thin knife edge, dulling it in minutes. Any chef will tell you that a sharp knife is safer (less likely to slip off whatever you're cutting), than a dull knife.

fectly produced Martini. If you want the ultimate olive garnish, you can either marinate oversized olives in vermouth for a few months, or you can hunt around for "tipsy olives" or "tipsy onions," which are packed in vermouth rather than regular brine. There are also olives stuffed with garlic, anchovies, blue cheese, almonds, even jalapeño peppers (*see page 73*).

There are two methods for cutting twists. Jared learned one at his first bartending job: a place that used $2.49 bottles of American "champagne" for their Mimosas. He was taught to cut the ends off the lemon, loosen the insides with a full twist of the bar spoon and push them out (easier than it sounds), and cut the resulting empty barrel in half lengthwise and then crosswise into twist strips. *Voila*, uniform twists and minimal waste.

He picked up the second method at the Rainbow Room in Manhattan while watching the service bartender set up for the lunch shift. He took only the freshest lemons, washed them gently, and pared as many large ovals of peel off the outside as he could by slicing the lemon from top to bottom, unconcerned that he wasn't getting 100 percent of the fruit. As a result, his twists were shaped like mini-potato chips, with mostly yellow peel and only the slightest bit of white underneath.

SERVING WITH STYLE

A big part of the Martini experience is the presentation: A perfectly clean, chilled Martini glass, a frosty shaker, the sound of the ice shifting inside it as the drink is poured slowly. This is what the cocktail is all about.

One final note. You can't make up Martinis in advance. The flavor fades in less time than it takes a conga line to make it around the dance floor. The taste goes perceptively flat, so don't mix them unless you're planning to drink them right away.

From this point on, you're on your own road to Martini Nirvana. We can't offer advice on which recipe to try first or last. That is a personal choice, one that each aficionado must make on his or her own. Be prepared for all sorts of advice–which reminds us of a story Bob Tucker sent us:

> The entire Royal Canadian Mounted Police carry a small survival kit with them at all times in a small leather, zippered case. Inside, there are miniature bottles of gin and vermouth. The kit also contains a small metal cup, a swizzle stick, and a card that instructs the Mountie: should he/she become hopelessly lost in the wilderness, they should sit down, take out the survival kit, and begin making a Martini. Before the drink is mixed it's guaranteed someone will appear to rescue them, saying, "No, no, that's not the way to make a Martini!"

CHAPTER ONE

TOP SHELF

The Rise and Refinement
of the Classic Martini

More intellectual duels have been waged over the Martini's origins than for any other cocktail (and just as many feuds over its preparation have parted close allies). However, there is a détente. All factions mutually agree, Martinis must be made and presented with style. Traditions die hard, and we're grateful that this singular golden rule is the point of difference between the drink known as the "elixir of quietude" and other alcoholic beverages, like shooters, coolers, umbrella drinks, and Jell-O® shots.

As in any rite of passage, neophytes must prepare for the initiation that takes them from the adolescent world of keg parties to the refinement of the Martini. Elders of this growing sect are well versed in the enigmatic questions of mixology; they faithfully practice the prescribed rituals both in public and private. They revere the drink's champions. They tell tales that have been passed down from generation to generation about the Martini's origins and its rise to elegance. They share the names and locations of sophisticated Martini shrines they've discovered along the way.

THE TOP TEN ALLEGED MARTINI INVENTORS

1. J.P.A. Martini, Paris, France, 1763
2. Parker's Saloon, Boston, MA, 1850
3. Professor Jerry Thomas, Martinez, CA, 1852 (or San Francisco, CA, 1860)
4. Harry Johnson, New York, NY, 1860
5. Heublein Company, Hartford, CT, 1894
6. Martini & Rossi, Turin, Italy, 1890
7. The American Bar at the Savoy Hotel, London, UK, 1910
8. Signor Martinez, Waldorf-Astoria Hotel, New York, NY, 1910
9. Martini di Taggia, Knickerbocker Hotel, New York, NY, 1910
10. Harry, Harry's New York Bar, Paris, France, 1911

GIN & SIN
CLASSIC GIN MARTINIS

What did the Dutch medical professor, Franciscus de la Boë (aka: Dr. Sylvius), unleash upon the world when he formulated *genever*–a kidney tonic–in his laboratory at the University of Leiden in 1650? And what prompted distillers like Bols and de Kuyper & Zoon to produce gallons of the professor's "Dutch courage"–a distillation of fermented barley, maize, rye, and juniper berries –which they sold in stoneware crocks? Those are questions that we won't pursue here. However, we do want to briefly trace gin's pre-Martini history.

We know that the French fell in love with the early elixir's juniper aroma, enhancing the recipe with a few more herbs and creating their own version: *genièvre*. And we must tip our hats to Great Britain's only Dutch monarch, William of Orange, who introduced *geneva* (eventually shortened to *gen*) to the English.

In London, ambitious distillers created a drier-tasting variation, adding more savory herbs and dubbed the resulting spirit dry gin. The locals went wild. Gin distilleries cropped up in towns and villages from Dover to Plymouth as the demand for dry gin grew. Manufacturers like Sir Felix Booth achieved fortune and fame thanks to dry gin. (Booth shared his wealth, contributing £17,000 to James Ross' Arctic Circle expedition in 1829. The explorer thanked his benefactor by naming the Boothia Felix Peninsula–the Canadian North-

Some great dry gins to try include: Bombay Dry, Bombay Sapphire, Plymouth, Board's, Boodle's, Booth's High & Dry, Tanqueray, Beefeater, Gilbey's, and Gordon's.

I'm tired of gin,
I'm tired of sin,
And after last night,
Oh boy, am I tired.
–Anonymous

London dry gin is flavored with more than a dozen different herbs and spices. Besides juniper berries, dry gin also contains bitter and sweet orange, cinnamon, bitter almonds, calamus, fennel, anise, caraway, lemon, cassia, and nutmeg.

west Territories' northernmost tip–after him.

By the time Queen Victoria ascended to the British throne, distillers like Bombay had spent over seventy-five years perfecting the blend of flavors as well as the slow distillation process in continuous stills. Unlike sweeter Old Tom gins, dry gin's flavor was more appealing to those who liked to pair their potable with an accompaniment like bitters or quinine tonic.

"Gin was mother's milk to her," Eliza Doolittle remarked about her aunt to a gathering of polite Victorians in George Bernard Shaw's play, *Pygmalion* (aka: *My Fair Lady*). London's gin palaces were filled with unemployed workers drowning their financial sorrows in local gin–often mixed with milk. More temperate citizens like Prime Minister William Ewart Gladstone tried to ban the spirit, and William Booth established the Salvation Army to free good men and women from the evils of "mother's ruin."

Government restrictions placed on the manufacture and sale of alcohol didn't stop people from drinking. It only improved the quality: distillers of cheap booze were put out of business if they couldn't afford the new production licenses. So only people who could afford to buy high-quality liquor could drink gin. It had become a "smart" drink among the social set.

PINK GIN

During the War of 1812, Londoners toasted Wellington's army with their national drink: dry gin. It was the heyday of England's gin history. Most Brits drank their potion "neat" (straight), but some well-to-do sippers poured their gin into a glass coated with the latest French and Italian import: vermouth. Gin-and-French and Gin-and-It were respectable drinks.

As the British Empire grew, Royal Army officers brought back more unique gin recipes. China Gordon drank gin slings (gin mixed with lemon juice and sugar) while he awaited his fate in Khartoum. Regiments stationed in India and Africa laced their malaria medication–quinine tonic–with an ample dose of gin. And the Royal Navy drank Pink Gin to relieve the digestive distress encountered in tropical climates.

In 1966, Sir Francis Charles Chichester reputedly drank Pink Gin while he sailed alone around the world in his 53-foot yacht, the *Gipsy Moth IV*. If you spent 107 days sailing non-stop from Plymouth, England, to Sydney, Australia, you'd certainly need fortification. (It must have been good. Chichester tackled the 119-day return trip sipping the same mix.)

Were Pink Gin and Gin-and-It the Martini's respectable ancestors? (Some Brits still use the term Gin-and-It when ordering a Dry Martini.) We pondered these primal origins as we crossed the English Channel to investigate a French source.

Let stand

4 oz. (120 ml)
Plymouth Gin

6 drops
Angostura Bitters

Coat the glass with bitters. Then add the gin until the liquid turns pink.

At one time, **Gin-and-It**–dry gin mixed with Italian dry vermouth –flowed freely at London gin palaces like the Red Lion on Duke of York Street near St. James Palace. Barmen coated a wine glass with dry vermouth before adding the gin. There were some customers, however, who preferred **Gin-and-French** which replaced Italian with French dry vermouth.

J.P.A. MARTINI'S MARTINI

ATTRIBUTED TO JEAN PAUL AEGIDE MARTINI

Let stand

2 oz. (60 ml)
genièvre

1 oz. (30 ml)
dry white wine

1 pinch
ground cinnamon

A few varieties of dry white wines to try include: Puilly Fuisse, Bordeaux Blanc, Fumé Blanc, and Sauvignon Blanc.

Good thing Martini changed his name. Can you imagine saying: "Hey, bartender. Could we get another round of extra-dry Schwartzendorfs?" So much for the three-Martini lunch, no one would have been able to say it after two drinks.

Johann Paul Aegius Schwartzendorf is the Martini's only alleged inventor who was not a bartender or beverage company. Born in Freistadt, Germany, on September 1, 1741, Schwartzendorf was a musical prodigy–by the age of ten, he was the organist in a Jesuit seminary. His biographers reported that the talented young Johann went home around 1758 and found a wicked stepmother installed at his family abode. Not amused by this change of events, the musician left home for good, seeking his fame and fortune in Nancy, France–even though he didn't speak the language and didn't have a penny to his name. Schwartzendorf was befriended by a local organ builder named Dupont who advised him to change his name to Jean Paul Aegide Martini. (Italian composers were in demand in those days.) Three years later, Martini hopped the fast lane to fame and fortune: He received the coveted position of court composer for King Stanislas, who was living at Lunéville.

His mentor died a few years later, but once again Lady Luck favored Martini, who became the toast of Paris by winning a heated competition to write a march for the Swiss Guard. He followed up that success by composing a number of popular light operas, a cantata written expressly for Emperor Napoleon's wedding ceremony, and by accepting an appointment as the conductor of the Théâtre Feydeau.

Despite his religious upbringing,

Martini was no different from his French art and music compatriots: He caroused and cavorted in the City of Lights' numerous taverns. One biographical account mentions that his favorite drink was a concoction made with *genièvre* and dry white wine. His friends dubbed this drink after its creator.

Unlike his many contemporaries who subscribed to the "live hard and die young" philosophy of most absinthe drinkers, the *genièvre*-drinking Martini lived to the ripe old age of seventy-five. According to the legend, after his death in 1816, Martini's drink was often requested by Montmartre musicians and artists who imported the recipe during the nineteenth century as they sought fame and fortune in the New World.

J.P.A. Martini's other alleged creation **Martini Verboten** consisted of 2 oz. (60 ml) genièvre and 1 oz. (30 ml) apple cider vinegar.

Back in J.P.A. Martini's day, colonial Americans ordered a slug, an eye opener, or a nightcap at a bar or tavern. Gin's nickname changed a few times from phlegm cutter (c. 1806) and firewater (c. 1817) to red eye or rot gut (c. 1819). Cheap gin earned the dubious title of blue ruin (c. 1831).

MARTINEZ

Shake

2 oz. (60 ml)
Old Tom gin

0.5 oz. (15 ml)
Martini & Rossi Extra-Dry
Vermouth

2 dashes
maraschino liqueur

3 drops
Bogart's Orange Bitters

lemon slice

While Thomas and Johnson were pouring fingers, snorts, nips, and pick-me-ups for their customers, gin was often called lush (c. 1840), coffin varnish (c. 1845), forty rod (c. 1858), tanglefoot (c. 1859), and tarantula juice (c. 1861).

Their happy patrons toasted their comraderie with a simple "Bottom's up."

Many historians have attributed the Martini's origins to Manhattan bartender Professor Jerry Thomas' creation: the Martinez. Curiously enough, in the 1862 edition of Thomas' *The Bar-Tender's Guide and Bon Vivant's Companion*, neither the Martini nor the Martinez are listed among the recipes. In fact, according to the editor of the 1928 edition, Herbert Asbury, "The first edition of the *Bon Vivant Companion* lists but ten different varieties [of cocktails]: the bottle, the brandy, the fancy brandy, the whiskey, the champagne, the gin, the fancy gin, the Japanese, the soda, and the Jersey."

Gin Cocktails and Fancy Gin Cocktails had been around since 1845, and Thomas' recipes were very similar to the Martinez, which he eventually added to his 1887 revised edition. Following the tastes of the times, Victorian cocktails usually contained sweeteners–sugar syrup, gum syrup, or liqueur–added to the individual's taste. Did Thomas invent these gin-based cocktails? Barmen at Parker's Saloon in Boston were shaking up gin cocktails in 1850. As far back as 1856, the Gin Cocktail was listed on the beverage menu at Mart Ackerman's Saloon in Toronto, Ontario. If Thomas had created the Martinez while working at the Occidental Hotel in San Francisco between 1860 and 1862, it's strange that he didn't include it in the book's first edition. So Thomas' story seems dubious. (But don't let the controversy stop you from making a pilgrimage to Martinez, California, as you can still get a pretty fine Martini there.)

Professor Thomas was quite a showman, pouring flaming Blue Blazers for his Manhattan clients. As Henry Asbury wrote in his 1928 introduction: "Aye, even in Europe [Jerry Thomas] was recognized as a master craftsman; he visited Liverpool, Southampton, London, and Paris in 1859 bearing with him his magnificent set of solid silver bar utensils constructed at a cost of $4000 for his own personal use, and astonished the effete drinkers of the Old World with the variety and extent of his virtuosity." We wonder if Thomas imported the Martini in the same way he introduced a celebrated British cocktail, the Tom & Jerry, as his own creation when he returned to America.

One of Thomas' contemporaries, bartender Harry Johnson, did not have that P.T. Barnum entrepreneurial spirit, but he did practice and teach mixology in New York. The first edition of his drink book, entitled *New and Improved Illustrated Bartender's Manual or How to Mix Drinks of the Present Style*, was self-published in 1882 and contained detailed instructions for both the Martinez and the Martini among a few hundred recipes, preparation, and presentation tips. According to some beverage historians, this was the first documented use of the name *Martini*.

Professor Thomas' **Gin Cocktail** mixed 2 drops Bogart's Orange Bitters, 4 oz. (120 ml) gin, 1-2 dashes Curaçao, and 3-4 dashes gum syrup (try Karo Syrup) served in a standard glass. The **Fancy Gin Cocktail** was made with the same ingredients but was served in a "fine wine glass." Both were shaken until ice cold and garnished with a lemon twist.

Harry Johnson's Martini mixed equal parts Old Tom gin and vermouth (about one-half wine glass of each) with 1 dash Curaçao, 2 dashes of Boker's Bitters, and 2 dashes gum syrup.

CLASSIC LIQUEURS, CORDIALS, AND SYRUPS

CHERRY:
maraschino, Cherry Heering, kirschwasser

CHOCOLATE:
crème de cacao

ORANGE:
Cointreau, Triple Sec, Grand Marnier, Curaçao, Punt e Mes

MINT:
crème de menthe, peppermint schnapps

POMEGRANATE:
grenadine syrup

Shake

2 oz. (60 ml) of each:
Plymouth Gin and Martini
& Rossi Extra-Dry
Vermouth

I dash
orange bitters

lemon twist and a green
olive

The olive garnish was re-
putedly added by Manhat-
tan bartender Robert
Agneau who used it to
conceal the raw taste of
American gin.

The **Knickerbocker**
—named after the Manhat-
tan hotel—adds 0.5 oz.
(15 ml) sweet vermouth
to di Taggia's signature
drink.

John Doxat, author of *Drinks and Drinking*, told a story about a Knicker-bocker Hotel bartender–Martini di Arma di Taggia–who allegedly invented the Martini in 1910 for his most famous customer, John D. Rockefeller. According to the story, the oil baron usually ordered Gin-and-French, but the barman offered him this orange-laced alternative. The Heublein Company was already selling pre-mixed Martinis; and Martini & Rossi was also given credit for its creation: a rumor perpetrated by author H.L. Mencken, instigator of a great media hoax about the origins of the bathtub, which a gullible public also swallowed whole.

One thing is certain, Martinis had truly gone to the dogs (or rather the dog show judges, as we shall see) years before Mr. di Taggia mixed them. The evidence is in the New York Public Library's menu collection. A Hotel Flanders banquet menu–dated November 22, 1899–for a Philadelphia Dog Show Judges' Dinner presented a first course of Blue Point Oysters and Martini cocktails. These lucky banquet guests also consumed Potage a la Reine served with Amontillado; Terrapin served with Roderer Brut 1893 champagne; Saddle of Venison served with Moët et Chandon Brut Imperial champagne; Roast Duck, Fried Hominy and Romaine Salad; Brie and Stilton cheeses; and a Bombe Glacé served with cordials. (And they wonder why we live longer these days.)

H.P.W.

They may dedicate monuments, libraries, even municipal swimming pools in your honor, but you know you've really found immortality when they name a drink after you. Martinis were all the rage at turn-of-the-century banquets, hotel bars, fancy dining rooms, and gentlemen's private clubs. One member of the esteemed New York Racquet Club was honored with a personalized Martini. Harry Payne Whitney had inherited his father's sizable financial interests and a serious love of horse racing. (He later lent his name to the art world: the Whitney Museum of American Art was named after him.)

The Racquet Club's renowned bartender, Charlie, was not going to have his patron nor his bar outdone by Rockefeller and di Taggia. This drier blend didn't garner as much attention locally –Americans preferred sweeter cocktails at the time. But the H.P.W. did gain the respect of London's dry-gin elite.

Shake

1 oz. (30 ml)
Plymouth Gin

2 oz. (60 ml)
Martini & Rossi Extra-Dry
Vermouth

orange slice

Gentlemen's club patrons used a few lively, but civil toasts like:
- Here's how
- Here's to you
- Here's looking at you

Author Rudyard Kipling had a hearty toast:
"Ship me somewhere East of Suez, where the best is like the worst;
Where there ain't no ten commandments and a man can raise a thirst."

The **Racquet Club**'s signature Martini added 6 drops Bogart's Orange Bitters to the same recipe.

The Old Army combined 2 oz. (60 ml) gin, 1 oz. (30 ml) Italian vermouth, 2 lemon twists, and an orange twist in the shaker. The concoction was garnished with a silver skin cocktail onion.

GIBSON

Shake

2 oz. (60 ml) of each:
Old Tom gin and Martini
& Rossi Extra-Dry
Vermouth

silver skin cocktail onion

The **Murphy** simply replaced the Gibson's signature cocktail onion with a raw radish garnish.

Our own version—the **Dirty Gibson**—combines 2 oz. (60 ml) Bombay Sapphire Gin, 1 oz. (30 ml) Martini & Rossi Extra-Dry Vermouth, 1 tsp. cocktail onion brine, and a silver skin cocktail onion garnish.

Ever wonder who invented the Gibson? It's the drink Roger Thornhill ordered in the dining car of the Twentieth Century Limited instead of his usual Martini in the film *North by Northwest*. There are a bunch of stories about the invention of the Gibson. Our favorite (and the most plausible) is that the Gibson is named after Charles Dana Gibson, a famous turn-of-the-century illustrator and creator of the Gibson Girls.

Legend has it that he liked to join his friends for happy hour cocktails at The Player's Club between 1891 and 1903. He also wanted to finish these outings with a clear enough head to return to his latest magazine cover illustration. He worked out a code with the club's bartender, Charlie Connolly: his Martini was nothing but ice water, and Charlie "marked it" by using a silver skin cocktail onion instead of an olive garnish. His friends quickly caught on—not to the code, but the garnish. Lauding his inventiveness, they ordered their Martinis with cocktail onions and named the variation after him. It's rumored that the double cocktail onion garnish was meant as a tribute to the physical assets of Gibson's beautiful models.

Another Player's Club guest, actor Cyril Cusick, took the Gibson with him to Murphy's Bar in Dublin where the owner (who was out of cocktail onions) stuck a radish in the drink instead. With that, the Murphy was born.

SIDECAR

Sometime around 1911, a Manhattan bartender named Harry moved to France, opening his own establishment in Paris's Second Arrondisement. Located at 5 Rue Daunau, Harry's New York Bar was a favorite haunt for cosmopolitan Parisians, the new wave of *nouveau riche* American tourists, and creative expatriates like Ernest Hemingway and F. Scott Fitzgerald searching for inspiration on foreign shores.

Harry's faithful following arrived by 11 A.M. for a round of the proprietor's breakfast Martinis made with Noilly Prat Vermouth. After a few eye-opening belts, patrons often switched to Harry's other signature cocktails: White Ladies and Sidecars.

Shake

2 oz. (60 ml) of each:
Boord's Gin and brandy

1 dash
fresh-squeezed lemon juice

Harry's **White Lady** was made with 2 oz. (60 ml) dry gin, 1 oz. (30 ml) Cointreau, 1 splash lemon juice, and 1 tsp. whipped egg white.

Located in Philadelphia, the **Clover Club** had a signature drink that replaced the Cointreau with 2 tsp. raspberry or grenadine syrup. The **Clover Club No. 1** used 1 splash grenadine syrup and 1 dash lemon juice.

The **Clover Leaf** shook the same ingredients plus 2 sprigs peppermint and a mint leaf garnish.

GLOOM RAISER

CREATED BY ROBERT AT THE ROYAL AUTOMOBILE CLUB

Shake

2 oz. (60 ml)
Booth's High & Dry Gin

1 oz. (30 ml)
Noilly Prat Vermouth

2 dashes of each:
grenadine and absinthe

lemon twist

One of London's famed "gentlemen mixers" was Robert, who worked at the Criterion and the Embassy Club between the World Wars and wrote his own book entitled, *Cocktails: How to Mix Them*. While he held court at the Royal Automobile Club (around 1915), Robert created the Gloom Raiser: the first of many signature drinks he created which included the Princess Mary (gin and crème de cacao topped with cream), a "hair of the dog" (hangover) remedy called a Gin Fizz for the morning after, and the Yellow Rattler, which he described as a "cowboys' cocktail."

Around the same time, bartender Harry MacElhone at Ciro's Club invented his own Yellow Rattler which he named the Monkey's Gland. No one is too sure why MacElhone gave it such an unusual name (it's obvious he didn't major in marketing), but no one seemed to mind ordering it either. It was "the drink" throughout London's trendy

West End and–once the war ended–on the sunny resort beaches of Deauville and in the nearby Monte Carlo casinos.

Robert's **Yellow Rattler** shared a great deal in common with the H.P.W. and the Gibson, consisting of 1 oz. (30 ml) vermouth, 2 oz. (30 ml) dry gin, 1 dash orange bitters, and a "small bruised white onion" garnish.

Harry MacElhone's **Monkey's Gland** was made with 1 oz. (30 ml) dry gin, 1 oz. (30 ml) fresh orange juice, 2 tsp. each of both grenadine and absinthe (or Pernod). In some circles, this drink was called a **Yokohama**.

Around 1921, a drink named after heavyweight boxing champ Jack Dempsey hit the sunny Deauville beaches. The **Dempsey** was made with 1 oz. (30 ml) dry gin, 2 oz. (60 ml) Calvados, 1 tsp. grenadine, and 2 dashes absinthe (or Pernod).

THE CIVILIZED APPROACH

So how do you hold a Martini glass? A friend said it best: "This depends. One bartender insisted that every Martini had to be as cold as his ex-wife's heart and held 'by the throat.'

"My former employer lifted his Martini with his pinky extended: a strangely dainty gesture for a gentleman built like a heavyweight wrestler. Later, I discovered that he'd broken his pinky and couldn't bend it. (I stopped imitating him.)

"One lounge femme fatale seductively suggested that I hold the stem gently between my thumb and forefinger, not high enough to feel the hard chill pulsing through it, but just where I can feel its dampness caress my fingertips."

Unlike a snifter which has a stubby stem and fits in your hand so that your body heat warms the contents (bringing its subtle flavors to life), a Martini glass is designed to keep your drink cold, but only if you hold it by the stem—not the bowl.

STAR

ATTRIBUTED TO IVOR NOVELLO

Stir

1 oz. (30 ml) of each:
Booth's Gin and Calvados

1 dash of each:
Noilly Prat Vermouth,
Martini & Rossi Extra-Dry
Vermouth, and grapefruit
juice

*Laugh and the world
laughs with you—drink
and it does the same.*
  —Tom Walls,
An Anthology of Cocktails

*H.L. Mencken, while
researching the etymology
of the word "cocktail" for
his monumental work*
The American Language, *hired a mathematician to
calculate how many dif-
ferent cocktails could be
mixed from the stock of a
first-class bar. The answer
was 17,864,392,788.*
  —John Watney,
  Mother's Ruin

The "Bright Young Things" who inhabited London and Paris after the First World War were part of a "lost" generation: rootless rich kids and wealthy young widows mostly, who were disillusioned by war. This live-for-today group drowned its intense despondency in Martinis and many of the roughly 7000 other cocktail variations that *Drinks and Drinking* author John Doxat estimated that Jazz Age barmen mixed for their clientele.

For those who couldn't afford to trip the light fantastic, hundreds of cocktail books taught the Lost Generation how to mix their own. *An Anthology of Cocktails, together with Selected Observations by a distinguished gathering, and diverse Thoughts for Great Occasions*—a booklet produced by Booth's Gin—was one notable contribution, presenting British theatrical, sports, and social celebrities, their endorsed signature recipes, comments, and anecdotes. Ivor Novello, West End theater idol and star of an early Alfred

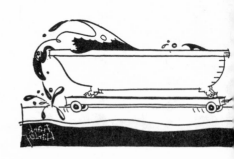

Hitchcock film, contributed the Star—the collection's smash hit.

It took a few years before the drink got rave reviews from Jazz Babies on the other side of the Atlantic. Prohibitionist Carrie Nation had started a grass roots movement in the 1880s, warning God-fearing Americans about the evils of liquor. The popular vote erred on the side of abstinence even though President Woodrow Wilson himself vetoed the concept. Also the passage of the Volstead Act and the U.S. Constitution's Eighteenth Amendment put a cork on the Cocktail Age's rising tide—above ground anyway.

The Nassau Gun Club in Princeton, New Jersey, made their own version of the **Star**, eliminating both vermouths and grapefruit juice.

The American bar in London's famed Savoy Hotel concocted their version—the **Rolls Royce**—by replacing the grapefruit juice with Benedictine.

The **Arnaud** (named after stage actress Yvonne Arnaud)—which was also featured in the Booth's booklet—was made with equal parts of dry gin, extra-dry vermouth, and crème de cassis.

THE BUFFALO HYPOTHESIS
(AN AS-YET UNPROVEN AND DUBIOUS THEORY)

A herd of buffalo moves only as fast as the slowest buffalo, much like the human brain operates only as fast as the slowest brain cell.

The slowest buffaloes are the sick and weak who fall victim to predators, making it possible for the herd to move at a faster pace.

Like the buffalo, the weak or slow human brain cells get killed off by excessive Martini drinking and socializing, making the brain operate stronger and faster.

The upshot: Party. It'll make you smarter.

Shake

2 oz. (60 ml)
Gordon's Gin

0.5 oz. (15 ml) of each:
Cinzano Dry Vermouth and
Rose's Lime Cordial

lime slice

Forty miles from whisky,
And sixty miles from gin
I'm leaving this damn
country
For to live a life of sin.
—Anonymous

Cocktails continued to flow in the hotels, casinos, and gentlemen's clubs in Paris, Berlin, and London. Europe had "free and easy drinking customs," American temperance leader Reverend Daniel Dorchester proclaimed at the start of the Roaring Twenties. Americans were forced underground (and abroad) in search of their Fizzes, Rickeys, Slings, and Martinis after the Eighteenth Amendment went into effect on January 16, 1920. The resulting prohibition on the sale and manufacture of alcoholic beverages did more than make outlaws out of upstanding American citizens, it birthed a new counterculture of mobsters, rum-runners, flappers, and playboys.

Many Americans devised ways to "sneak a belt of the sauce." Rum-runners criss-crossed the Canadian border and bathtub gin makers brewed up moonshine-quality hooch for a thirsty American public. Designer hip flasks became common fashion accessories. Smoky speakeasies—where the underworld rubbed shoulders with rich café society—and some savvy restaurateurs had ingenious ways of outsmarting law enforcers, serving cocktails in coffee cups and constructing hidden panel bar shelves.

Even a few Ivy-League undergraduates applied their knowledge of chemistry to quench their desires, distilling their own bootleg liquor. But there was a hitch. Without the controlled conditions and secret botanical formulae used by large-scale distillers, bathtub gin

tasted more like liniment than liquor. (These amateur chemists were blending industrial alcohol with glycerine and juniper oil.) Princeton University's student body developed some palate-soothing solutions, adding sweetened lime juice, port wine, or orange bitters to their Martinis.

Restaurant business declined when the stock ran out around 1922, but Prohibition bolstered the membership and attendance at private clubs. The bastions of the social elite had discreetly ordered and concealed a fourteen-year supply of imported liquor before the law was enacted because members happily footed the bill to ensure their favorite "poison" was on hand during hard times.

Lost Generation artists and intellectuals seemed to have great connections to the underground liquor supply. It was during this time that *New Yorker* book reviewer Dorothy Parker wrote her Martini dedication:

According to Groucho Marx, W.C. Fields kept about $50,000 worth of booze stashed in his attic: "Don't you know that Prohibition is over?" Groucho asked. "Well, it may come back!" Fields replied.

Named after a hit Noël Coward play, the **Fallen Angel** blends 2 oz. (60 ml) Gordon's Gin, I oz. (30 ml) lemon juice, and a half-teaspoon crème de menthe.

"I'd gotten all set up for a day of fishing," the old angler said to his friends. "Found a perfect river-bank under a willow tree, had a cooler with all the fixings and made myself a perfect Martini, when I realized I'd forgotten to bring bait. Just then I spotted a small snake with a big minnow in its mouth slithering out of the water. I caught it and took the minnow to use for bait. But I felt so guilty about stealing the snake's breakfast that I poured a few drops of my Martini into his mouth before I let him go. Half an hour later I felt something against my leg. I glanced down, and here's that same snake, back with three more minnows."

I love to drink Martinis,
Two at the very most
Three, I'm under the table
Four, I'm under the host.

It may have started as a one-hour roast of New York theater critic Alexander Woollcott, but the infamous ten-year-long lunch of the Roundtable at New York's Algonquin Hotel ignited the intellects of the rebellious young generation. Critics like Parker, playwright George S. Kaufman, writer Robert Benchley (who is often credited with saying, "I must get out of these wet clothes and into a dry Martini"), Woollcott (also credited as originator of the same quote), and playwright/songwriter Noël Coward (who focused his plays *The Vortex* and *Fallen Angels* around the subject of cocktails) gathered daily for lunch to hurl memorable innuendoes and venomous insinuations and to drink Martinis in the upstairs room where the Roundtable's Thanatopsis Club played poker. (It wasn't against the law for people to possess liquor in their homes or hotel rooms.) They also adjourned to Tony's—a speakeasy on West Fifty-second Street—or the original "21" Club—which was called the Red Head when it was located in a Greenwich Village house before moving to its famous Midtown location.

Cocktails played an important role in the group's gatherings at their private retreat—Neshobe Island in Vermont. "Dinner on the island was only part of the evening ritual," Roundtable member Harpo Marx recalled. "The first ceremony at day's end, for which everybody gathered in the clubhouse, was Cocktails."

An occasional Roundtable guest, novelist P.G. Wodehouse, also contributed a few Martinis to the era's literature, creating characters like the amiable British playboy Bertie Wooster who braced himself for every formal dinner with a couple of dry Martinis prepared by his valet Jeeves, a master mixologist.

It was hard to stop the general public from enjoying themselves, despite the fire-and-brimstone preaching, ax-wielding teetotalers who had lobbied for Prohibition. Funny thing about that law: it didn't actually ban the purchase and consumption of alcoholic beverages, just their manufacture and sale. All the booze that people had bought beforehand (or claimed they had) could be given away legally.

This gave birth to thinly-veiled schemes like the "Blind Pig." A beer garden or outdoor bar would be set up. Patrons would pay fifteen cents to get a look at a blind pig or some other non-attraction held in a corner of the bar. Of course, a free drink was included with every admission. Luckily, one American politician took a stand in 1933, signing the order to repeal the Eighteenth Amendment so the gin could once again flow freely in American streets and in his own home: the White House.

A popular Prohibition toast was "Here's mud in your eye!"

Not to be outdone by its New Jersey counterparts, **Yale** University students didn't dilute their gin with vermouth. They added 3 dashes orange bitters and 1 dash Angostura Bitters to their gin.

A post-Prohibition version of the **Princeton** blended 2 oz. (60 ml) Old Tom gin, 1 splash port wine, 2 dashes orange bitters, and a lemon twist garnish.

A non-academic variation —the **Hudson River** —mixed equal parts of gin and apple cider with 1 dash Angostura Bitters and a roasted almond garnish.

A popular elixir among Jazz Babies who frequented Chinatown speakeasies was the **Hong Kong Special**: equal parts of gin and Noilly Prat Vermouth, 1 dash Angostura Bitters, and bar sugar to taste.

When the quality of gin improved, patrons ordered the **Bennett**: 3 oz. (90 ml) gin, 1 oz. (30 ml) lime juice, and 1 dash Angostura Bitters.

DIRTY MARTINI

Shake

1.25 oz. (37.5 ml)
Plymouth Gin

1.75 oz. (52.5 ml)
Argentine vermouth

1 tsp.
olive brine

stuffed green olive

Rub the glass rim with a
lemon twist before pouring
and garnishing.

Appropriate toasts to FDR's
favorite Martini include:
- Happy days are here
  again!
- To the New Deal!
- To the Working Man!

Ever wonder what it was that made Franklin Delano Roosevelt such a popular U.S. President? Okay, so there was the New Deal, the end of the Great Depression, his pro-workingman approach to domestic policy, his warm and accessible public persona, and his remarkable personal strength as demonstrated in his determination to overcome physical challenges. But Roosevelt also signed the order to repeal Prohibition, shook the first legal post-Prohibition Martini, and had a talent few commanders-in-chief possessed. Perhaps Noël Coward put it best:

> [Roosevelt's] study was typical of him, I think. It was furnished unpretentiously and in quiet taste...his desk was solid and business-like, although at the moment it had banished affairs of state for the day and given itself up to frivolity, for it was littered with an elaborate paraphernalia of cocktail implements. There were bottles, glasses of different sizes for short and long drinks, dishes of olives and nuts and cheese straws, also an ice bucket, a plate of lemons with a squeezer, a bowl of brown sugar, two kinds of bitters and an imposing silver shaker. Among all these the President's hands moved swiftly and surely; they...never erred,

whether he happened to be looking at what he was doing or not. He was evidently proud of his prowess as a barman, as indeed he had every reason to be ...

Roosevelt brandished his cocktail shaker for heads-of-state and distinguished guests throughout his terms in office. He personally favored Old Fashioneds and Dirty Martinis, but according to some sources, he occasionally strayed by adding a splash of orange juice, grapefruit juice, or anisette to his Martini.

When I joined [FDR] in his study for cocktails I was relieved to see that there was no apparent change in his manner towards me; he offered me a dry Martini without contempt.

—Noël Coward

I didn't know what a Dirty Martini was, but two very attractive women a few seats down from me at the bar ordered a few rounds. Each time they gave the bartender a lascivious wink and a smile. Certain I had stumbled on some sado-sexual secret society's signal I watched out of the corner of my eye as he mixed a round for them. Sure enough, he ladled a spoonful of some unrecognizable clear liquid from below the bar into their glasses. I guess they spotted me, because they told the bartender to make one for me, too. Caught! I was tempted to make a run for it, but curiosity got the best of me. Don't know if I was more relieved or disappointed to discover that it was just a standard see-through with extra olive brine. However, it makes for a darned good Martini!

THE ASTORIA

Shake

1 oz. (30 ml)
Old Tom gin

2 oz. (60 ml)
Noilly Prat Vermouth

2 dashes
Abbott's Orange Bitters

Other 1930s inventions like **The Polo Mallet** added 1 dash Angostura Bitters and a silver skin cocktail onion garnish to the Astoria recipe.

The **Crest o' the Wave** replaced the orange bitters with Angostura Bitters, 6 drops crème de menthe, and a peppermint cherry garnish.

The **Blenton** combined equal parts of gin and vermouth with 1 dash Angostura Bitters.

Thanks to President Roosevelt, the Cocktail Age went into full swing on American shores during the remainder of the 1930s. Cocktail lounges and nightclubs sprouted up nationwide, replacing saloons as social gathering centers. The public couldn't afford to drink a lot, but they did want memorable cocktails to wash away their Depression blues. Bartenders like Oscar at New York's Waldorf-Astoria Hotel and Robert at London's Criterion Club, developed elaborate specialty cocktail menus with a myriad of Martini variations.

Railway companies hired professional barmen to serve travelers in their elegant club cars. The Orient Express wasn't the world's only deluxe passenger train. Playwright/composer Noël Coward frequently toured the U.S., taking the Twentieth Century Limited from New York to Chicago and the Super Chief from Chicago to Los Angeles. Like his fellow passengers –millionaires, actors, and writers–Coward reveled in the quality of the American rail service commenting:

> The over-luxurious journey from New York to Chicago in the 'Twentieth Century'; the red carpet laid across the platform; the obsequious coloured porters in their white coats; the deep armchair in the club car; the superlatively dry dry Martini before dinner; the dinner itself, perfectly served and of such infinite variety so far removed from the sullen

table d'hôtes of our own dear Southern [British] Railway...

But the flourishing cocktail culture wasn't limited to licensed establishments, Pullman rail cars, and hotel lounges where these professionals held daily court. Art Deco cocktail cabinets, fanciful cocktail shakers, various sizes and shapes of glassware, swizzle sticks, and other mixing paraphernalia were just as important to a well-furnished house as couches, arm chairs, and dinnerware. A gentleman's ability to mix a Martini for guests in his home was a symbol of civility; of a person who knew how to appreciate the finer things in life; of a person who could rise to the top of his profession.

For those who preferred a sweeter drink, bartenders offered patrons a **Sweet Martini** made with 2 oz. (60 ml) gin, 0.75 oz. (22.5 ml) sweet vermouth, and an orange twist garnish. Sometimes the vermouth was replaced with marsala or sweet sherry.

The **Merry Widow** was made with the same amounts of gin and Dubonnet Blanc plus 1 dash orange bitters.

A **Flying Dutchman** added 1 splash Curaçao to the standard gin and vermouth blend.

Shake

3 oz. (90 ml)
Old Tom gin

0.5 oz. (15 ml) of each:
Martini & Rossi Extra-Dry
Vermouth and Martini &
Rossi Sweet Vermouth

*Who the hell put ice in
my Martini?*
—Vicky Ocean,
Very Vicky Comics

Another popular Martini variation served in the 1930s was the Bronx –named after the New York City zoo. It had been around since the First World War, and there were as many versions as there were appellations to this particular blending of gin with both dry and sweet vermouths. In the 1932 drink book *The Art of Mixing*, author John H. Wiley named his balanced blend of equal parts gin and Italian and French vermouths the Lone Tree.

Bartenders at the Nassau Gun Club in Princeton, New Jersey, added 1 splash freshly squeezed orange juice or an orange section to their **Gun Club Bronx** before shaking. Other professionals called this version a **Bronx Express**.

A simple, but not so plain variation—combining 2 oz. (60 ml) Booth's Gin, 1 oz. (30 ml) each of both Noilly Prat Vermouth and orange juice, and 4 dashes Curaçao—paid homage to the American cowboy philosopher and actor **Will Rogers**.

Appealing to the ladies both for its name and its formula, the **Chorus Lady** blended equal parts gin, dry and sweet vermouths, freshly squeezed orange juice, and an orange slice garnish.

Since its creation, the preferred ratio of gin to vermouth in a Martini has radically changed. Belle Époque Martini aficionados ordered an equal balance of gin and Italian dry vermouth topped with a dash of orange bitters. During the Depression, sippers requested two parts gin to one part vermouth. (There were holdouts at the Nassau Gun Club who continued to order a Perfect Martini: "a mixture of one part Italian vermouth and one part of French vermouth with three or four parts of gin, with the usual dash of bitters." But its popularity waned in favor of stronger, drier formulae.

One explanation for the drying of the Martini is that the quality of American gin improved. Vermouth–usually the lesser-priced and lower-alcohol ingredient–made for a cheaper, lighter drink. Consequently, less vermouth made for a more exclusive and stronger beverage.

Martinis got progressively drier as the Second World War began. Fashion gave way to subjectivity in maturing public tastes. Extra-dry Martinis–a 4:1 blend–were succeeded by the 8:1 formula served at 1950s three-Martini corporate lunches. Today it's not uncommon to find modern aficionados ordering what author Ernest Hemingway called a Montgomery–a 15:1 super-dry Martini–in his novel *Across the River and into the Trees.*

"Two very dry Martinis," [Colonel Cantwell] said. "Montgomerys. Fifteen to one."

Stir

2 oz. (60 ml)
Gordon's Gin

1 oz. (30 ml)
Martini & Rossi Extra-Dry
Vermouth

1 dash
Bogart's Orange Bitters

stuffed green olive
or lemon twist

The Blue Bar at the **Algonquin** Hotel replaced the bitters with Pernod in their signature Martini.

Call my mother…dinner at "21," seven o'clock. I'll have had two Martinis at the [Plaza Hotel's] Oak Bar. So she needn't smell my breath.
—Roger Thornhill,
North by Northwest

During the 1930s and 1940s, a **Medium Martini** combined 2 oz. (60 ml) gin, 1 oz. (30 ml) each of both French and Italian vermouth.

Author Ernest Hemingway preferred desert-dry **Montgomerys**: 3 oz. (90 ml) gin to 1 tsp. Italian vermouth.

Patrons of the Nassau Gun Club liked their **Perfect Martinis** blended according to a truly classic formula: 4 oz. (120 ml) gin, 1 oz. (30 ml) each of both French and Italian vermouth, and 1 dash Bogart's Orange Bitters. More daring drinkers ordered a **Pall Mall**, adding 1 tsp. white crème de menthe to the shaker.

The **Boomerang** also made its way around cocktail parties, mixing equal parts of gin, French and Italian vermouths, 1 dash Angostura Bitters, and a maraschino cherry garnish.

The waiter [at Harry's Bar in Venice] who had been in the desert, smiled and was gone....

Hemingway had named the variation after Field Marshal Bernard Law Montgomery, leader of the British Eighth Army during the Second World War's North African campaigns. The story goes that Monty would only attack Nazi General Ernst Rommel–the Desert Fox–and his men if His Majesty's forces outnumbered this formidable foe by a 15:1 ratio.

Some modern Martini drinkers prefer an even drier blend: or "only the shadow of the vermouth bottle" or a quick spritz of vermouth. (Remember, if you're going to fill a perfume or cologne atomizer with vermouth make sure it's clean–after all, you don't want to go down in history as the inventor of the Calvin Klein's Obsession Martini, do you?)

V FOR VICTORY

ADAPTED FROM WINSTON CHURCHILL'S RECIPE

During the 1940s *blitzkrieg*, Londoners who wanted to escape the ravages of the Second World War sipped Martinis made with Noilly Prat Vermouth between the nightly bombing raids. But unlike his contemporaries, British Prime Minister Winston Churchill drank his Martinis naked–without even the slightest hint of vermouth. His drinking and cigar-smoking prowess were as legendary during wartime as his victory symbols–the first four notes of Beethoven's Fifth Symphony and the two-finger "V." In fact, Churchill often loosened his tongue with a couple of stiff Martinis before entering into one of his notorious dinner battles with Parliament Member Lady Astor.

Cocktails were a staple in the Churchill family diet long before Winston took to drinking. Lady Sara Churchill–the Prime Minister's American mother–had invented and imported the Manhattan to British shores.

A **Naked Martini** relies totally upon presentation. Shake up either your favorite gin or vodka with plenty of ice. Strain and pour into a chilled glass and garnish with a lemon twist.

Shake

3 oz. (90 ml) Plymouth Gin

lemon twist

Pour the gin into a shaker filled with ice. Shake until it's ice cold, turn toward the direction of France and bow before straining.

In one of many famed verbal sparring contests between them, Lady Astor, his daughter-in-law and also a Member of Parliament, remarked to Churchill at a dinner party, "You're drunk!" "And you," he reputedly replied, "are ugly. Now tomorrow morning, I shall be sober."

Shake

5 oz. (150 ml) Plymouth gin

lemon twist

Pour the gin into a shaker filled with ice. Shake until it's ice cold. Tap a bottle of extra-dry vermouth against the shaker three times before straining.

I never go jogging, it makes me spill my Martini.

—George Burns

The **Deano** (aka: **Dean Martini**) is 4 oz. (120 ml) dry gin served with a Lucky Strike cigarette and a book of matches.

Particular about his actors (and even more so about his selection of actresses), British film director Alfred Hitchcock was another critical Martini drinker who preferred to have his gin uncluttered by the taste of vermouth. His stout build could have been partly due to his grand consumption of food and drink between projects, but as Hitchcock himself commented:

> There seems to be a widespread impression that I am stout. I can see you share my amusement at this obvious distortion of the truth. I may loom a little larger just now, but you must remember this is before taxes.

For all of you calorie-counting imbibers, here's a breakdown:

calories	fat (g)	cholesterol (g)
2 oz. Medium Gin Martini		
151	0.0	0.0
2 oz. Extra-Dry Gin Martini		
142	0.0	0.0
2 oz. Extra-Dry Vodka Martini		
129	0.0	0.0

A Martini can obviously hide its svelte form in the shadow of a 262-calorie Piña Colada, a 215-calorie wine cooler, or a 174-calorie Screwdriver in the battle of the bulge. Stuffed olives and cocktail onions add on about ten more calories, a few more vitamins—and in the case of olives, 0.2 g of cholesterol. But if caloric count is your only concern, the good news is that twists don't add weight to your drink.

THE EMPIRE MARTINI

CREATED BY PAUL THE BARTENDER

There are even pros that pursue the ultimate arid blend. In San Francisco, Paul the Bartender pours his Empire Martini. Doug Varnes at Set 'Em Up Joe in Chicago "polishes" his double Martinis with a light vermouth spray. But there are ways to get even drier. Chris Madison told us about another barman:

While living in Los Angeles in the mid-1970s I witnessed an interesting "twist." There was a most obnoxious man who came into my favorite lounge everyday at precisely six o'clock and ordered two Extra-dry Martinis for him and his female companion. He complained every time that they were not dry enough. Those of us who were regulars would rib the bartender after the man left, until the afternoon when the bartender pulled this stunt:

Shortly before "Mr. Extra-dry" arrived, the bartender placed a small bar towel in the bottom of the metal shaker. (None of us saw him do it.) When Mr. E showed up and ordered, the bartender casually set up the shaker, and poured the ice and gin in full view of everyone. He then took the vermouth bottle and waved it around the shaker. "That should be dry enough, don't you think?" the bartender asked. Mr. E concurred. Then the bartender poured. The bar towel had absorbed the gin so only a drop or two of liquid came out. "Is that dry enough for you?" he asked. Needless to say, Mr. E was rather astonished and promptly left. Mr. E, by the way, never came back.

Let stand

3 oz. (90 ml)
gin blend
(50/50 blend of Gilbey's
and Boord's)

3 atomizer blasts
vermouth blend
(75/25 blend of Noilly
Prat Vermouth and
Cointreau)

fresh Spanish olives

Freeze the shaker and glass in advance. Only the gin gets placed in the shaker with ice and left to stand while you spray the vermouth into the glass. Then strain the mix into the glass.

Overheard: "No. No. I mean *really* dry! I want to see the dust on my olives."

THE PERFECT HATFIELD MARTINI

CREATED BY CRAIG HATFIELD

Stir

2 oz. (60 ml)
Bombay Sapphire Gin

1 splash
Martini & Rossi Extra-Dry
Vermouth (optional)

Thoroughly chill both the glass and the gin in the freezer. Pour the gin into the glass and either add a splash of vermouth or simply wave the bottle over the glass. If you do add vermouth, gently stir the mixture with a glass pipette to avoid "bruising."

Roll a plump Spanish olive down the side of the glass for garnish.

I had never tasted anything so cool and clean. They made me feel civilized.

–Frederic Henry,
A Farewell to Arms

Not all aficionados search for the world's driest Martini; most concern themselves with perfection. A few classicists insist that a Martini should be stirred rather than shaken because it bruises the gin. We don't know exactly how the rumor got started. (There's certainly ample proof that Victorian and Cocktail Age mixologists shook their blends.)

This rumor seems to have originated in the cocktail lounges and taverns frequented by 1950s corporate execs, who measured up their competition by observing their opponent's ability to hold two or three strong drinks. It's easy to point to classic bar manuals that only recommend shaking for certain drinks, and claim that others are stirred to avoid "bruising." But the truth is, they just didn't bother to shake a drink that wouldn't become frothy. Many of the drinks they did shake, we now make in a blender and wouldn't dream of shaking.

We did extensive testing–shaking versus stirring various ratios–and couldn't detect a difference in the flavor. Shaking does impart more water to the drink. But we definitely found a better blend and quicker chill by using this method.

Unless you've got a home-crafted, sediment-filled vermouth, shaking shouldn't affect the fragrance inherent in high-quality gin nor the Martini's finished flavor. Besides, if you use bar-style speed-pourers on your bottles, the liquids are already getting knocked around before they hit the shaker.

On November 22, 1995, the Discovery Channel asked Discovery Connection quiz competitors–professors from the University of Manitoba and Carleton University–a bonus question:

According to scientists, shaking a Vodka Martini…

1. does nothing to alter the drink.

2. excites the alcohol molecules to jump down your throat.

3. increases the alcohol concentration.

4. causes tiny bubbles to make the taste less oily.

5. oxidizes molecules called aldehydes to make the taste sharper.

The answer was choices 4 and 5.

A regular walked into his local bar, but when the bartender pulled out a shaker, the customer grimly shook his head. "Just a glass of water. Doctor said I have to cut out the Martinis and eat more vegetables." The bartender shrugged sympathetically and gave it to him. The customer downed the water in a gulp, pulled out a jar of olives and dumped them into the empty glass. "I tell you what, though. I think my vegetables would like a Martini."

The Martini has a way of making instant friends out of people, some of whom become, uh, more than friends. We had an incident [at the 1994 Seattle Martini Competition] where right out in front of the building, this couple…in front of all of us. Then a guy walked into a wall, apologized to it, and walked away.

—Marc Nowak

A SOCIAL MARTINI

CREATED BY SARA LENNARD

Makes four servings

Shake

6 oz. (180 ml)
Beefeater Gin

2 oz. (60 ml)
Noilly Prat Vermouth

stuffed olives

Shake the gin and vermouth on ice. Let sit. Shake again and strain into 4 Martini glasses.

As this drink's creator instructed: "Always...serve another before dinner."

Our own **Double Tradition** mixes 2 oz. (60 ml) gin, 1 oz. (30 ml) French vermouth, and 1 dash Angostura Bitters. Garnish with two olives. Then repeat the process.

Some folks drink Martinis as their pre-dinner stimulant, exciting the appetite and shrugging off the workday stress before the entrées arrive. But pragmatic mixologists like John Burra have discovered a way to make entrées out of their Martinis: "Have your Martini up [or] on the rocks with your favorite gin. Just spear an olive, small mushrooms, and a cocktail onion. Stir and eat. Color can be added by using a twist of lemon and lime on each end."

One word of caution, Martinis can have some surprising social contraindications if consumed in quantity without a sumptuous meal. The Mayflower Park Hotel's Marc Nowak told us a story that illustrates the potential dilemma:

This couple was sitting at the bar. She was having a Martini, he was drinking a beer. This other woman came in, and the two ladies began to argue. The first one stood up, poured her Martini down the other woman's blouse and stormed out, with the man following close behind. They were still arguing outside. I overheard him saying something like: "I've put those clothes on your back," at which point she started taking them off, right in the street; and in nothing but her underwear she marched down the street. All over a Martini, and straight out of a Fellini movie.

THE BERLIN STATION CHIEF

CREATED BY JEFFREY CARLISLE & CHARLES WHARTON

Inspiration can be divined from recent literary sources. Carlisle and Wharton of The Policy Hut in Washington, D.C., created a refined Silver Bullet (a Martini made with Scotch instead of vermouth) based on a passage from author Norman Mailer's 1991 novel *Harlot's Ghost*:

> [William King Harvey] mixed a batch of Martinis: He filled the shaker with ice, poured in a quarter inch of scotch, poured it out, then loaded the pitcher with gin. ... "The scotch adds that no-see-um flannel taste you're looking for. Slips the job down your gullet," [he commented.] He drank off his first fill, gave his another, and passed me one. It did slide down. Smooth fire, sweet ice. I had the disconnected thought that if I ever wrote a novel I would call it *Smooth Fire, Sweet Ice*.

A **Golden Triangle Station Chief** uses a blended scotch like Chivas Regal or Crown Regal.

A **Paraguay Station Chief** uses Bombay Gin rather than Bombay Sapphire.

A 1930s **Paisley** employed an extra twist: a splash of extra-dry vermouth or Kina Lillet Blanc.

The **Miller**—created by Pete Miller—uses 4 oz. (120 ml) Bombay Sapphire Gin, 1.5 oz. (45 ml) extra-dry vermouth, 1 drop Macallan Scotch, and a large—with or without pit—olive garnish.

Shake

2 oz. (60 ml) Bombay Sapphire Gin

0.5 oz. (15 ml) Lagavulin Scotch

lemon twist

Pour the scotch over the ice, swirl to coat, and then casually strain. (If seems wasteful, use less scotch and don't throw it out.) Add the gin and shake. Rub the twist around the bottom of the glass. Strain and pour the mix. Let stand for a few seconds, and then discard the peel.

Some other great scotches to try include: Macallan, Carhu, Glenmorangie, Glenfiddich, Glenlivet, and Laphroaig.

I should never have switched from scotch to Martinis.

—reputedly, Humphrey Bogart's last words

THE VIRGIN MARTINI

Shake

**3 drops
Angostura Bitters**

ice

**3 stuffed green olives or
lemon twist**

You can avoid tennis elbow from excessive shaking: add 2 oz. (60 ml) mineral water, lemon-lime soda, or lemonade.

Trying to explain the meaning of the word oxymoron? *Virgin Martini* is not a bad place to start.

It was summer, and we were on our way to attend a wedding ceremony at the Bogus Basin Ski Resort near Boise, Idaho. After renting a four-wheel drive at the airport, we stopped off to fortify the passengers for the long, twenty-mile drive up that the rental agent had cautioned was winding, steep, and boring. It was Friday night at the local hotel lounge, but we managed to squeeze onto a few barstools.

We were on our second round (everyone except the designated driver), when a very pretty–but obviously underaged–young woman wandered up to the bar. The bartender offered her a Virgin Martini. It certainly got our attention!

He placed a cocktail glass filled with ice and water on the bar to chill, then spilled it out. He dropped two olives into the glass, wrung out a lemon twist over the top, and discarded the rind. Then he filled a shaker with ice, affixed the lid, and began to shake. He shook, and shook, and shook. Finally, he poured the contents into the glass and slid it across the bar to the girl. "Now drink it in good health," he said with a wink to us, "and come back in a few years."

But seriously. Since so much of what makes up a Martini is the show of meticulous preparation, a Virgin Martini is not completely impossible. The right glass, proper service, and the right garnish is all it takes. If you're not pouring the VM's main ingredient (water) out of liquor bottles, try to come up with some decent glass or crystal decanters to set the stage. After all, so much of the Martini's appeal is its inherent romance; the alcohol is almost secondary. Also, make sure whoever is bartending wipes the rim of each glass with a lemon twist: a trick we learned from a bartender who made nearly virgin Martinis himself.

Bitters? In a Virgin Martini? In any Martini? Obviously, most early Martinis recipes contained bitters. Angostura Bitters, the best known of all, was invented in 1824 by a Prussian Army surgeon who'd gone to Venezuela to join Simon Bolivar's forces in the liberation of South America. Created in the town of Angostura, his gentian root concoction still bears its name.

We recently went to buy a bottle of Angostura Bitters. (No, we didn't finish ours, we'd misplaced it). We wandered up and down the supermarket aisles before we gave up and asked the manager. He led us to the check-out counter, opened a locked cabinet, and pulled out a bottle. When we asked why he kept them hidden, he explained that people had been taking them off the shelves, gulping them down (after all, it is 90 proof) and leaving the empties behind. Have you ever tasted straight bitters? These people should have been easy to spot: writhing across the floor with their faces sucked in so far they could hide behind a dime. We asked if he had the same trouble with Chinese cooking wine (grain alcohol, water and a little salt). No one ever touched it. Go figure.

Did you hear the one about the couple who'd been together so long they were on their second bottle of bitters?

FROM RUSSIA WITH LOVE
CLASSIC VODKA MARTINIS

Medieval western Europe was a dark, dreary place. The Black Death and the Crusades weren't the worst of it: gin hadn't been invented yet. But twelfth-century Russians, Poles, and Czechs were a pretty cheery bunch despite the long, cold winters. They had a blood-cleansing, enervating tonic called *zhinznennia voda*–"the water of life." It was simply a distillation of fermented winter wheat (not potatoes, as some historians would have you believe), charcoal-filtered to remove both aroma and unappealing flavors. But it was such a mouthful to say–especially after reaching the state of alcoholic stupor known as *zapoi*–that the spirit was eventually given a more endearing name: vodka ("the dear, little water").

As Prince Vladimir of Kiev was quoted in the medieval tome, *The Russian Primary Chronicle*: "Russians are merrier drinking–without it they cannot live." But eight centuries later, vodka wasn't given its own classification like scotch or gin in the United States. It was a just a little better known than Cynar. (Haven't tried Cynar? It's an artichoke liqueur.) This elixir owes most of its rising popularity and overwhelming success in the West to six people.

The first key figure was Pierre Smirnoff, who opened his Moscow distillery in 1818. Using improved distillation and a double-filtration process, Smirnoff's vodka gained the public's admiration. And in 1886, Smirnoff became imperial purveyor to the Romanov household. (The czar's annual vodka consumption totaled up to more rubles than his Fabergé egg purchases!) When Russia entered the First World War, vodka-making was banned and the Smirnoff descendants fled into exile. The Bolsheviks wanted the people to be sober; so hard-drinking Constructivist artists and writers had to settle for bootleg booze. The ban was eventually lifted in 1925 to stop the widespread illegal, and often lethal distillation.

Around that time vodka's second and third key figures met in Paris. Vladimir Smirnoff–Pierre's exiled descendant–befriended Rudolph Kunett, a naturalized Ukrainian-American who missed vodka. He purchased Smirnoff's name and the right to produce the spirit in the United States–after Prohibition was repealed, of course. Kunett opened the American Smirnoff distillery–located in Bethel, Connecticut–in 1934, but the business failed. Russian products and culture were blacklisted in the minds of the pro-capitalist American public, and Kunett sold his interests to the Heublein Company in 1939.

During the 1950s, a novel and a bottle of ginger beer led to vodka's rise. Jack Morgan, owner of the Cock 'n Bull Tavern in Los Angeles, had gotten a taste for ginger beer on a trip to England. When he returned home he tried his hand at producing his own brew. He made barrels of it, but there were no takers. So he played with different combinations until he hit on the Moscow Mule: a long drink made with vodka and ginger beer. It was an immediate hit with

Some great imported Russian vodkas to try include: Stolichnaya, Stolichnaya Gold, Moskovskaya, Star of Russia, Priviet, Starka, Smirnoff Black, and Kremolyovskaya.

Other great vodkas to try include: Fris, Finlandia, Absolut, Tanqueray Sterling, Ketel One, Smirnoff Blue, and Skyy.

Q: Should you eat the olive first or last?
A: First. It's not healthy to drink on an empty stomach.

Californians, who carried it across the nation.

Former British intelligence agent and journalist Ian Fleming published his first novel in 1952. He'd borrowed the main character's name from a book on tropical birds written by an author named James Bond, and gave the secret agent some of his own personal tastes, including one for Martinis–Vodka Martinis. During the Second World War, Fleming lamented the slump in quality at his favorite London watering hole, The American Bar at the Savoy Hotel:

> When I tell you that the Savoy Hotel are [sic] now mixing Martinis out of bath-tub gin and sherry you will know that we are rapidly progressing back to swamp life and the transitional period is distasteful.

Fleming's James Bond thrillers were immediate bestsellers throughout the Cold War. And Bond's Martini preferences became a symbol of sophistication, especially in the wake of the blockbuster motion pictures that followed in the 1960s.

During President Jimmy Carter's term in office, the three-Martini lunch was viewed as a negative perk; a devious tax deduction taken by fat-cat corporate types. Something had to be at fault. The nation was in the midst of a severe recession at that time. Hard liquor drinks were out and frozen fruit drinks, wines, and beer were in during the 1970s. Both gin and vodka were "establishment" beverages, consumed by straight-laced corpies, not by the hip, leisure-suit and disco-dress crowd. Despite this, in 1975 vodka replaced scotch as America's best-selling spirit. After a decade, the public thankfully grew up and turned its attentions toward more sensible potables.

In the midst of the high-powered 1980s, the final key figure brought vodka to prominence as

Europe and North America's highest-selling distilled spirit. Michel Roux, President and CEO of Carillon Importers, Limited, led the campaign by accentuating vodka's elegance and sophistication, branding the spirit's inherently versatile and creative nature at a time when people demanded the best of everything. Vodka was a natural choice. The public craved quality options from a wealth of international sources: the best Belgian chocolates, the finest French cognacs, the smokiest single malt scotches, and the strongest, iciest Russian vodkas.

The stresses of the "lean and mean" 1990s coupled with the increased demand for tasteful amounts of concentrated quality (versus gallons of fat-laden mediocrity) have fueled vodka's continued appeal. Although Vodka Martinis don't have the lineage of their gin cousins, they are a firmly-established, modern symbol of taste.

PARDON ME, BARTENDER.
MY MARTINI'S TOO COLD

A perfectionist once asked if he could chill a Martini with liquid nitrogen. It reminded us of this passage from Martin Cruz Smith's novel, *Polar Star*.

The year before, an Intourist guide had taken a group of Americans into the [Siberian] taiga and laid out an even more splendid lunch but had forgotten to turn the [vodka] bottle. After many toasts with warm tea...the guide poured glasses of nearly frozen almost congealed vodka and showed his guests how to drink it in one go. "Like this," he said. He tipped the glass, drank it and fell over dead. What the guide had forgotten was that Siberian vodka was nearly two hundred proof, almost pure alcohol, and would still flow at a temperature that would freeze the gullet and stop the heart like a sword. Just the shock was enough to kill him. It was sad, of course, but it was also hilarious. Imagine the poor Americans sitting around the campfire, looking at their Russian guide and saying, "This *is* a Siberian picnic."

BURNS ON THE ROCKS

ADAPTED FROM GEORGE BURNS' RECIPE

An interviewer asked comedian George Burns if he felt like he was slowing up at the age of ninety-three. He replied: "I've noticed a few signs, for instance....When I blow smoke rings I've noticed they're smaller and not as round as they used to be. And when I drink a Martini, instead of two olives, I'm down to one." Burns considered his Vodka Martini on the rocks as much a part of his daily ritual as playing cards, smoking cigars, exercising, and taking an afternoon nap. During his century-long life, Burns knew all the big show people: George Jessel (who allegedly invented the Bloody Mary because he hated the smell of potato vodka), Dean Martin, Frank Sinatra, and W.C. Fields (who drank two pre-breakfast double Martinis daily).

One story goes that Burns ran into Fields after Fields was ordered to go on the wagon. Fields explained: "Well, George, my dear friend, your source is impeccable. It's quite true I'm not drinking anymore....However, I'm not drinking any less either."

Journalist Hugh Pickett recalled one backstage visit in 1986 that proves our point:

> George was in his Tux pants, and his white shirt, making Martinis, and I can vouch for it, they were lethal. I had two, so did he, and then he went out and wowed a sold out house, never missed a beat, or a step when he tap-danced.

Stir

2 oz. (60 ml) Smirnoff Vodka

0.5 oz. (15 ml) Noilly Prat Vermouth

lemon twist

Pour vodka into a rocks glass filled with ice, then add vermouth, stir 3 times, and serve.

Make mine a Vodka Martini, straight up. Oh, and with an olive.
–George Burns, *18 Again*

Our own **Lucky Martini** mixes 3 oz. (90 ml) vodka with 7 drops French vermouth. Stir gently 7-11 times in a clockwise direction. Garnish with 3 chilled gambling dice.

THE VESPER
ADAPTED FROM IAN FLEMING'S RECIPE

Shake

3 oz. (90 ml)
Plymouth Gin

1 oz. (30 ml)
Moskovskaya Vodka

0.5 oz. (15 ml)
Kina Lillet Blanc

lemon peel

We served Vespers to our New Year's Eve guests in red-wine goblets which captured the drink's distinctive citrus edge, and made it tougher to spill (which they still managed to do after one or two).

Just like his nineteenth-century Victorian predecessor Sherlock Holmes, Bond epitomized modern sophistication and savoir-faire. A notorious litera-a-day vodka-drinker himself, Fleming introduced Bond's impeccable taste in food and drink throughout the pages of his first thriller, *Casino Royale*.

The Vesper–named after the story's heroine Vesper Lynd –was Bond's (and Fleming's) personal recipe for a Medium-Dry Vodka Martini. The choices of vodka and vermouth were important, too: grain vodkas (Russian) were preferred over potato vodkas (Polish). Kina Lillet Blanc (a French aperitif similar to vermouth) replaced popular Italian vermouths like Cinzano or Martini & Rossi. Bond insisted his cocktail had to be shaken not stirred until ice-cold, and served with a large slice of lemon peel in a champagne goblet.

Although the Vesper was never mentioned again (when Vesper died, the name seemed to die with her), Bond did imbibe Martinis in other novels and in almost every one of the nineteen films starring Sean Connery, George Lazenby, Roger Moore, Timothy Dalton, or Pierce Brosnan in the starring role.

Why has Bond remained so popular in a time when trends emerge and fade weekly? Because he embodies the desire for quality, taste, and adventure that modern men and women seek amid the chaos and stress of their daily lives. As James Bond said in *Casino Royale*: "I never have more than one drink before dinner. But I do like that one to be large and very strong and very cold and very well-made. I hate small portions of anything, particularly when they taste bad." It's hard to disagree with that.

Our personal adaptation is named the **From Russia with Love**. It blends 1 oz. (30 ml) Bombay Sapphire Gin, 2 oz. (60 ml) Stolichnaya Gold Vodka, and 0.5 oz. (15 ml) Kina Lillet Blanc according to Bond's precise directions. Naturally, it's shaken until it's ice cold and garnished with a lemon twist.

Merchant's in New York devised a **James Bond Martini**: 3 oz. (90 ml) Tanqueray Gin, 1 oz. (30 ml) Smirnoff Vodka, and 0.5 oz. (15 ml) Kina Lillet Blanc. Rinse the ice with Martini & Rossi Extra-Dry Vermouth before the ingredients are added to the shaker.

> *"A dry martini," [Bond] said. "One. In a deep champagne goblet…Three measures of Gordon's, one of vodka, half a measure of Kina Lillet. Shake it well until it's very cold, then add a large thin slice of lemon peel. Got it?"*
> —Ian Fleming, *Casino Royale*

LUCKY JIM
ADAPTED FROM KINGSLEY AMIS' RECIPE

Stir

2 oz. (60 ml)
Smirnoff Vodka

1 tsp.
Cinzano Dry Vermouth

1 splash
cucumber juice

cucumber slices

Happiness is a Dry Martini and a good woman…Or a bad woman.

—George Burns

Lola's serves a **Joe Average** made with 2 oz. (60 ml) Stolichnaya Vodka and 1 splash Pimm's No. 1 Cup (an herb flavored gin) garnished with a cucumber slice and a lemon slice.

Outspoken and irreverent, British novelist Kingsley Amis shared a love of dry Martinis with his friends Ian Fleming and John Doxat, preferring a 15:1 formula. Another common bond between Amis and Fleming was James Bond: after Fleming passed away, Amis wrote a Bond adventure in 1968 entitled, *Colonel Sun* (under the pen name Robert Markham) as well as Fleming's biography–*James Bond Dossier*–in 1965.

Amis' first novel, *Lucky Jim*, was a rousing success when it was published in 1954. Jim wasn't suave or sophisticated, he was comic anti-hero undergraduate at a provincial university. Amis dedicated a cocktail to his character in his drink book, *On Drink*, commenting that Jim "would probably make his Clement Freud [sic] face if offered one, but he would be among the first to appreciate that its apparent mildness might make it an excellent love-philtre to press on shy young ladies, if there are any of these left anywhere in the land."

Tatou in Manhattan makes a **Tatouni**, using 3 oz. (90 ml) Ketel One Vodka, splashes of Martini & Rossi Extra-Dry Vermouth and cucumber juice, topped with a cucumber slice garnish.

THE PASINI EXPRESS

CREATED BY STEFANO PASINI

Not every Vodka Martini lover is a celebrated performer, novelist, or fictional character, but they all pay homage to the personal style and selectivity that the drink commands. When Stefano Pasini sent us this recipe he noted: "Have some good, tasty food afterwards...(I hope J.B. [James Bond] would appreciate this cocktail. But Felix Leiter would be even more enthusiastic.)"

Felix Leiter–the CIA agent that teamed up with Bond as he battled megalomaniacs like Dr. No and Mr. Big–was no neophyte to fine spirits. He was the embodiment of the debonair American man: cool under fire, loyal to his friends, and a connoisseur of regional cuisine. This Haig & Haig drinker surprised Bond when he ordered a medium-dry Martini with a twist made without the requisite orange-flavored Kina Lillet Blanc. "Domestic stuff," Leiter explained. "New brand from California. Like it?" Bond had to admit it was the best vermouth he'd ever tasted.

We've never found a California vermouth and neither has Pasini, but it hasn't diminished our respect for Felix Leiter or his vermouth expertise in the least.

Stir

3 oz. (90 ml)
Absolut Red Label Vodka

1 oz. (30 ml)
Martini & Rossi Extra-Dry
Vermouth

Pour the vermouth into a shaker full of ice. Shake for 2 seconds, then drain. Pour the vodka over the ice. Stir the mixture for no more than 30 seconds.

Some dry, white vermouths to try include: Noilly Prat, Martini & Rossi, Cinzano, Boissiére, Stock, and Kina Lillet Blanc.

Our version of **The Twist** mixes 2 oz. (60 ml) Smirnoff Citrus Twist Vodka and splashes of Kina Lillet Blanc and Stolichnaya Pertskova with a garnish of lemon and lime twists. (See *Distilled Essences* on page 118.)

A DOSAGE OF VERMOUTH

Vermouth gets its name from the German word for wormwood: *vermut*. It's a traditional ingredient found in both vermouth and absinthe. This fortified, flavored wine originated as a digestive aid in seventeenth-century Italy (similar wines date back to ancient Rome). Red wine was combined with additional alcohol and stomach-soothing volatile herbs like wormwood, juniper berries, coriander, orange peel, cloves, nutmeg, quinine—as many as forty different flavorings which have a short life once the bottle is opened. (Never buy a large bottle of vermouth if it's going to sit around for a few months. It quickly loses its character just like any other wine that's had a chance to breathe.)

French vintners introduced a drier formula made from Chardonnay and Sauvignon Blanc wines which was initially marketed throughout Europe by Noilly Prat in 1812. About a quarter century later, the Italian distributor Martini & Rossi marketed a sweet, red-hued vermouth. And in 1872, Lillet Fréres began producing their unique blend of fortified white Bordeaux with its distinctive orange undertone.

As an apéritif, vermouth is often thought to be too sweet and feminine. But real men sometimes drink it straight. Take Ernest Hemingway's hero, Frederic Henry, in *A Farewell to Arms*, for example. While convalescing in an army hospital, Henry offers his night nurse and confidante, Miss Gage, a vermouth. When she returns with the bottle and a glass, he says, "You take the glass. I'll drink from the bottle."

THE STELMACH MARTINI

CREATED BY STEVE STELMACH

A 99.44 percent pure Vodka Martini like the Stelmach Martini is the perfect liquid base for taste-testing a few new garnishes. Martini drinkers can't live by liquid alone, they must have garnish! But if you're tired of munching on pimento-stuffed green olives (and pickled pearl onions) there are alternatives.

Try a Buckeye–a Vodka Martini with a black olive garnish–or a Boston Bullet–a Martini garnished with an almond-stuffed green olive. You can also find olives marinated in vermouth, habañero peppers, mesquite smoke flavoring, Jamaican jerk seasonings, or wine. Mixologists we've met have stuffed their olives with everything including garlic, capers, anchovies (a Mariner's Martini), jalapeño peppers, blue cheese, cocktail onions, and smoked baby octopi (an Octopus Martini).

We do have one word of caution if you plan to stack your olives on a toothpick: make sure you don't consume the implement along with your veggies. (Author Sherwood Anderson made that literally fatal mistake while partaking in his daily Martini meal.)

Shake

2 oz. (60 ml) Stolichnaya Vodka

3 drops Martini & Rossi Extra-Dry Vermouth

stuffed green olive

Besides thoroughly chilling the vodka in the freezer, the ice should be made with filtered water.

The ingredients should be placed in a freezer-chilled glass shaker with a metal top, and shaken 20 times. Strain and pour the mix into glasses.

The olive should be rinsed under cold water to remove all excess oil before it's added.

If stuffed green olives don't appeal to you, then try the **Buckeye**: simply garnish a Vodka Martini with a black olive.

To make a **Boston Bullet,** simply garnish a Vodka Martini with an almond-stuffed green olive.

Shake

2 oz. (60 ml)
Suntory Juhyo Shochu
(vodka)

1 oz. (30 ml)
Gekkeikan Sake

lemon twist

If you're timid about trying anything new when you're abroad, order Daniel Dvorsky's **Extra-Dry and Slightly Bruised**: 6 oz. (180 ml) imported Russian vodka shaken until ice cold with 1 drop lemon juice.

Even though Japan produces some very fine liquors, not all Asian booze is up to that level of quality. Remember what James Bond said in *You Only Live Twice*: "Ugh. Siamese Vodka."

Too bad no one's published an update of Ian Fleming's travelogue, *Thrilling Cities*. Filled with recommendations from James Bond's creator, the book documented the finest places to drink and dine (circa late 1950s) in cities like Hong Kong and Tokyo.

If Hong Kong was your destination, Fleming recommended a visit to the Mexican bar in the Gloucester Hotel, which had the "best and biggest Martinis in the colony."

The intrepid author lunched with novelist Somerset Maugham (another famous Martini drinker) at the Imperial Hotel's Old Imperial Bar in Tokyo, but seemed to have missed their Martinis. (Thirty years later, we found them to be outstanding.) He also never ventured into unknown territory like tasting Saketinis, green-tea-laced Japanese Martinis (*see page 112*), Sakuratinis (*see page 107*), or Midori Martinis (*see page 93*). However, James Bond and Dikko Henderson drank their Martinis at the Hotel Okura's "Bamboo Bar" (which left Henderson with a royal *futsaka-yoi*–hangover–the morning after).

In fact, our own adventures in Tokyo yielded even more pleasant results. While staying at the Hotel Okura (right across the road from the American Embassy), we called room service. On a dare, we ordered two Martinis and hung up before they could ask any questions. Imagine our elation when two extra-large, perfectly chilled Vodka Martinis crafted with superb Russian vodka arrived!

Downstairs in the Highlander Bar, we found over two hundred brands of scotch. (Some day we might take out a second mortgage so that we can afford to try them all.) But, now we know why former President George Bush, Madonna, and other western dignitaries stay there.

Further investigations yielded similar surprises in the neighboring Ginza, Akasaka, and Roppongi districts. Bars like Henry Africa and the Americana shake up admirable Martinis.

While you're there, don't be afraid to try a few domestic vodkas. The travel book we used said vodka is "ouadka." We're still not sure what that translates to, but every time we said it the waiters would hold a conference until they'd reached a consensus that they had no idea what we were saying. Two words they definitely knew: "Stoli" and "Absolut." For local vodkas, we liked Suntory Juhyo Shochu and Hakutake Junmaisei Kuma-shochu.

If you're heading for Asia, here are a few toasts:
- Bali & Indonesia: Selamat!
- China: Yam sing! (Cantonese); Taiwan: Gun Bi!
- India: Aap ki shubh kai liyai!; Pakistan: Jama Sihap!
- Japan: Kan pai!
- Korea: Deupstita!
- Thailand: Chai yo!

TRANSOCEANIC MARTINI

CREATED BY FREDRIK AHLINDER

Let stand

**4 oz. (120 ml)
Stolichnaya Gold Vodka**

lemon twist

As Ahlinder explained, "The driest Martini ever is the one I poured myself back in Sweden. I called my friend in Australia, and asked him to shake the vermouth bottle near the telephone.

The sight of all those expensive cars rolling along, crammed to the bulwarks with overfed males and females with fur coats... made him feel that he wanted to buy a red tie and a couple of bombs and start the Social Revolution. ...Well, there is, of course, only one thing for a young man to do... Mervyn hurried along to the club and in rapid succession drank three Martini cocktails.
—P.G. Wodehouse,
Mulliner's Nights

The Transoceanic may sound suspiciously similar to a glass of vodka, though by local Swedish habits the mere addition of a twist nearly makes it into a lemonade. There are long traditions of serving straight spirits in northern Europe. Perhaps it's because in the depths of a Swedish winter anything with as little alcohol as vermouth is liable to freeze.

However, due south there are some fine establishments with a long Martini-making history. American bars (the European name for cocktail lounges) first appeared at the turn of the century. Unlike beer gardens, pubs, wine bars, and gin palaces, American bars specialized in American-style cocktails (which means they were served cold instead of at room temperature). Some of these bars were even owned by expatriate American bartenders.

The American bar at the Savoy Hotel in London–an early Hemingway hangout–still boasts that they are the Martini's birthplace. One British aficionado, Matthew Rose, suggested that "for anyone looking for a lesson in Martini etiquette, you must see Peter Dorelli, the head barman at the Savoy. Having mixed Martinis for thirty-four years he has a fair idea what he is talking about. Always Beefeater, Martini & Rossi–dry, of course–and a tiny squeeze of lemon oil from the fleshy part of the skin."

Le Dépanneur and Harry's New York Bar in Paris offer elegant settings and drinks that are guaranteed to take you back to the days when Ernest Hemingway, Cole Porter, George Gershwin, and F. Scott Fitzgerald took their seats to partake in a morning round of Harry's Martinis.

In Venice, there's another Martini shrine that was frequented by Hemingway: Harry's Bar which was owned by Giuseppi Cipriani. But be forewarned if you're headed down the Italian coast. As Stefano Pasini puts it: "There aren't many good Martini lounges in the famous Italian resorts...for example, the bar at the Hotel Posta in Cortina has served only a very watered shadow of a Martini in the last few years."

Schumann's Bar in Munich is reputed to have the best Martinis in Germany. And Chez Jean-Pierre in Copenhagen has distinguished itself among travellers headed for Scandinavia–home of Akavit and a variety of fine vodkas.

You certainly won't be disappointed if you're headed to Moscow. The hotel bars at the Metropol, National, and the Savoy serve up pre-revolutionary decor, excellent vodka selections, and perfect presentation.

Here are a few toasts to use if you're in Europe:
- Austria/Germany: Prost!
- Denmark: Skaal!
- Great Britain: Cheers! (general) Here's mud in your eye! (Cockney), Propino tibi! (Oxford or Cambridge)
- Ireland: Slainte!
- Italy: Cin Cin!
- Russia: Na Zdorovia!
- The Netherlands: Proost!
- Yugoslavia: Ziveli!

Ernesto Paez, an Argentine living in Copenhagen, devised a potent concoction–the **Argentine-Arctic Kick**–blending 3 oz. (90 ml) freezer-chilled 50/50 blended vodka (Finlandia/Stolichnaya), garnished with 2 stuffed green olives marinated in Martini & Rossi Extra-Dry Vermouth. (He suggested eating the olives before pouring the vodka. Keep them in your mouth for a few seconds before swallowing.)

The **Vesuvio Martini** made at a San Francisco landmark, Vesuvio's Café, is made to the same arid extremes as the Transoceanic. The difference is the garnish: a stuffed green olive.

Our own version–**The Seattle**–mixes 2 oz. (60 ml) Stolichnaya Gold and 1 dash fresh lemon juice. Freeze the cocktail glass with a few drops of Angostura Bitters. Before pouring the mix, mist the glass with vermouth from an atomizer to simulate the city's prevailing weather conditions. Then pour in the mix.

Shake without ice

2 oz. (60 ml)
Stolichnaya Gold Vodka

0.5 oz. (15 ml)
Retsina Blanc

lemon twist
or lemon-cured olive

This particular recipe requires no ice. A chilly, rushing body of water—a babbling brook, a white-water river, a glacial stream or lake—will do just fine. (However, we don't advise trying this at the ocean or in the Great Salt Lake.)

For those of you who've never tasted Retsina, this bone-dry Greek wine is still aged in pine casks just as it was thousands of years ago (with a little pine tar added, just in case your taste buds don't understand subtleties), so it takes on the flavor of the great outdoors.

Ah, camping season! The time when real men, women–and even lowly house pets–forsake the comforts of civilization (Martinis excepted, of course), and head for the untrammeled depths of the wilderness. Happy campers that we are, we assembled only the barest essentials: tents, air mattresses, sheets, comforters, pillows, three-burner stove, stainless steel pots and pans, enamel dinnerware, cutlery, glassware, a black leather port-a-bar, cellphone, laptop computer, cameras, binoculars, sunblock, bug repellent, citronella candles, flashlights, and gold-sifting pans. We popped over to the local Hertz office, rented a Ford Explorer, and set out to get close to nature in the alpine beauty of Nairn Falls just above Whistler, British Columbia.

So how do you chill a Martini on the second day when all the ice in the cooler has melted? Mountain glaciers around us beckoned. All that ice–but alas, just out of reach. We remembered something W.C. Fields said, "Once…in the wilds of Afghanistan, I lost my corkscrew, and we were forced to live on nothing but food and water for days."

We dove into the rushing Green River to cool off. It was a nice hot day, but somehow, if that water hadn't been moving so fast, it would've frozen solid. A shock wave of inspiration transpired. We duct-taped the lid onto a full shaker, cast it out on a few feet of twenty-pound fishing line we'd been using to

scare off the brook trout, *et voilà*! Shaken and chilled!

But we do have a word of recent experience: Never tape a wet shaker (with apologies to those drunken fish). One fishing tale is never enough, so here's one Coreen Larson told us:

It was another blazing hot summer day on the Canadian Prairies. Some friends and I decided that the only way to cool off was to try our hand, line, and luck at fishing. The prospect of spending four and a half hours floating around a calm and beautiful lake with a boatful of notorious beer drinkers was bittersweet. The moment reeked of a dry Martini and I knew it, but what could I do in the wilderness? I had to think fast.

Luckily, I came prepared. In an old tin lunch box, I packed a tiny little mickey of Tanqueray (I knew that mickeys were good for more than just drunken nights at high school dances), a jar full of vermouth (don't tell Noilly Prat), six green olives in a mini-Mason jar, a travel-size cocktail shaker, and a bucket full of ice on the side. All this with the essence of

Try a seaman's drink that's guaranteed to trim your sails: substitute a whole anchovy or an anchovy-stuffed olive for the Nairn Falls garnish. Dave Kaspryzk calls this one a **Mariner's Martini**.

The **Octopus Martini** at Ken Stewart's Grille uses a smoked baby octopus and a lemon twist garnish.

Dean Martin and we were "gone fishin"...woo wee!

Just when I thought it couldn't get any better–me with a full Martini, my Len Thompson hook dangling in the water and the sound of roaring motor boats and jet-skis singing quietly in the background–something happened that was orgasmic in proportion. I felt a tug on my line (if you know what I mean) and felt what had to be the biggest fish in the world trying to ingest my Len Thompson! I had to make a choice, and for the first time in my life, I gave up my Martini to reel in my catch. I handed it faithfully over to my fishing partner, Bartley Melnechenko, and had him hold my glass to my lips as I frantically tried to reel in the first fresh water shark in Saskatchewan!! Though my heart pounded and my physical and emotional strength faded, I felt tranquility with every new sip of martini. It was pure ecstacy.

Time stood still as I pulled in that weighty load. At times I felt like I was making no progress with the aquatic beast, but the gin restored my confidence. I'll never forget that moment on Child's Lake that August afternoon. The sun, the friends, the dry martini with two olives–shaken not stirred–and the "one that got away."

Even if you're stuck in the city, surrounded by nothing more exotic than pigeons, poodles, and the occasional potted plant, the Nairn Falls is sure to answer the call of the wild.

OLIVER'S CLASSIC MARTINI

CREATED AT OLIVER'S AT THE MAYFLOWER PARK HOTEL

When we first put up our Web site, one visitor wrote to us asking about the Seattle Martini Competition. We'd never heard of it and put out an all-points-bulletin for more information. After a few months, we finally tracked down the event's founder, Marc Nowak, who explained why he started it:

> In 1991, there was this place down the street named Vaughn's that had a giant banner on it saying: "BEST MARTINIS IN TOWN." Our customers would walk in and say: "Their Martinis are terrible, yours are much better." Anyway, we challenged them but, they wouldn't play! (Guess they didn't want to lose their banner.) So we challenged them in the press. They still wouldn't play.
>
> By this time, we decided to make it an open challenge. Boy, we got takers. The Four Seasons was in there in about two seconds; the Met Grill was another first challenger. Plus, we had a bunch of other restaurants. We narrowed it down by reputation and taste tests, figuring we could manage five, which [with two Martinis at each place] was a mistake, and ended up cutting it down to four bars the year afterwards. It's just grown from there. The first time [in 1992], we had sixty people, now there are hundreds. And it's turned into a very black-tie affair. It's a riot!

Oliver's at the Mayflower Park Hotel has won the award for Best Classic Martini four out of five times. After tasting it ourselves, we know why.

Shake

3 oz. (90 ml)
Stolichnaya Gold Vodka

1 oz. (30 ml)
Cinzano Dry Vermouth

vermouth-marinated stuffed green olives

Pour the vermouth into a glass shaker. Swirl to coat, and then drain. Fill the shaker with ice. Pour vodka over the ice and shake. Let stand for about 20 seconds. Place olives in a chilled glass and pour.

Gin aficionados shouldn't despair, Oliver's also makes this classic recipe with Bombay Sapphire Gin.

MOLOTOV COCKTAIL

CREATED BY LOLA OF LOLA'S AT CENTURY HOUSE

Shake

3 oz. (90 ml)
Stolichnaya Vodka

0.5 oz. (15 ml) of each:
Jameson's Irish Whiskey
and Irish Mist Liqueur

In all our research we've encountered plenty of drinks that are ignited before they're served, but we never came across a single flaming Martini. There are two good reasons not to. First, and most obvious: fire is hot, Martinis should be cold. And second, you generally make a Martini out of the best ingredients you can afford; surely there's something of less value that you can set on fire.

Not to be confused with the gasoline bottle garnished with a bit of rag, this drink is a far more sociable beverage capable of igniting lively conversation and a hint of the blarney. However, born pyromaniacs do need a little more satisfaction from their Martinis than the subtle smoky hint found in Irish whiskey. Steve Starr has a flamboyant option for their consideration:

This was first demonstrated to me by a bartender named Kimon at the Lion Bar in Chicago. I was there fifteen years ago and ordered a Martini with a lemon twist. Kimon asked me if I wanted it "smoked." It was a little noisy and I couldn't understand what he was saying, so I just said yes.

You make a regular Martini (preferably, in my opinion, with gin and straight up) in a classic glass. It must be ordered with a lemon peel garnish. Now, before you drop the lemon peel in the Martini, the lemon peel should be held two to three inches above the glass, light a match, then crisply and quickly twist the peel. If done correctly, there will be a brief but spectacular "*poof*" of flame and a little smoke. Immediately drop the lemon peel into the Martini. This adds a very subtle but yet distinctive smoky texture to the drink.

In essence, the Smoked Martini is half show and half taste. The lemon peel should have just a touch of the inner lemon (not just the rind) attached to it. The real tricky part is to be able to do the Smoked Martini by yourself. Holding the match and the lemon peel in just the right way allows you to [squeeze] the lemon peel and at the same time bring the lit match right [in front of the yellow side of] the peel as it twists, resulting in the flameout. At first, though, it's probably necessary to have a friend help by holding the match while you twist the peel or vice-versa, just so you can see what the effect should be.

Here's how this works. Lemon oil–which is trapped in the pores of the lemon rind–is highly flammable. (No, this doesn't mean that your lemons are likely to spontaneously combust and blow the door off the refrigerator.) When you squeeze a twist, it sprays little bits of oil out. Don't point the twist toward your eyes, even without a lit match, because the oil stings. Each twist is only good for one spray. After that, any oil that was destined to fly has already done so (although flaming the second squeeze is a safe way to practice your technique). This only works with fresh lemons. That shrunken yellow thing in the bottom of the fridge has already lost its oil–and flavor–to dehydration.

To make a **Smoked Martini**, blend your favorite classic recipe, but before you garnish the drink with a lemon twist, hold the peel over the drink, squeeze the twist and simultaneously light it with a match. When it finishes its flameout, drop the twist into the drink.

This is the ideal drink for any budding David Copperfield. For that complete Siegfried and Roy presentation, use an oversized twist and play Arthur Brown, Jr.'s 1960s hit song, "Fire."

SHAKEN NOT STIRRED

CHAPTER TWO

SPECIALS

The Modern
Martini Renaissance

For people in their twenties and thirties, Martinis are symbols of rebellion. Many of our parents–flower children that they were–tuned in, turned on, and dropped out. So what does Gen-X have as a social icon? They could all grow long hair, drop acid, and listen to psychedelic music. But their folks would drop by and proudly say: "That's my rebellious kid!"

You figure if they could tolerate grunge, then what's a hip parent's worst nightmare? It's that their kids would grow up to become conservative Martini-snobs who listen to lounge music, or worse–disco. The befuddled elders could call an exorcist. But let's face it, the only cure for a good Martini is another one.

Marc Nowak, founder of the Seattle Martini Competition, waxes more philosophically:

> There's a lack of romance in our culture today. We spend so much time working and running from one place to another, that by the time you're done you've forgotten what it's all about. When chivalry gives way to equality, everybody becomes a unit. The Martini goes back to an age when romance was good: opening doors for people, lighting someone's

I'm not talking a cup of cheap gin splashed over an ice cube. I'm talking satin, fire, and ice; Fred Astaire in a glass; surgical cleanliness; insight and comfort; redemption and absolution. I'm talking a Martini.

—Anonymous

cigarette, whatever. Those were the things that went with Martinis, and they still do. It brings back that era.

Second, it's pure. It's not that foo-foo stuff that baby boomers drank just after college. It comes in a glass that you can't slam on the bar twice and then shoot it. It's a very elegant drink. It's something you sip. It's a matter of taste. And we're growing up.

Mom may know her dry Chardonnays, and dad's been making boutique-quality home-brewed lagers for years. Sex is risky. Drugs are out, and rock 'n roll causes permanent hearing loss (to quote Pete Townshend, "Sorry, could you speak a bit louder?"). The Martini is the perfect classy and cultured counterpoint to a world where every day seems to be "casual day." And if they mistake it for nostalgia, make your next see-through a Glacier Blue (*see page 91*) or a Lava Lamp (*see page 99*). This is the new generation of Martinis!

GARDEN OF EDEN
FRUIT MARTINIS

Proponents of this Martini renaissance have enriched our treasury of folklore, enhanced our mixing rituals, and challenged Luddites who refuse to accept the drink's inevitable evolution. (That camp proclaims that the cornucopia of modern fruit-bearing variations aren't even distant Martini cousins.) But that's like comparing a Serengeti elephant to an Ice Age woolly mammoth. The evolution is pretty obvious. Strangely, no one denies that the sweet, orange-flavored 2:1 Martini was the great-grand-parent of the 4:1 Dry Martini.

We personally take a fully Darwinian view of the Martini. Just as it never followed one simple recipe and has changed over time, it's still changing.

NICK CHARLES:
Barkeeper, bring Mrs. Charles 240 Martinis. We won't be long.
—Shadow of the Thin Man

NICK CHARLES:
[to Nora] Swing it sugar. I've got a sleeper in the first. It's a honey.
NORA CHARLES:
I'll be with you in two shakes of a cocktail.
NICK CHARLES:
Cocktail? Cocktail? I think I'll try one of those things.
—Shadow of the Thin Man

LOLA

CREATED BY LOLA OF LOLA'S AT CENTURY HOUSE

Let stand

2 oz. (60 ml)
Stolichnaya Vodka

1 splash of each:
fresh orange juice, fresh
grapefruit juice, and
Cointreau

orange wedge

Gin can be used in place
of vodka.

The tall, elegant blond who tends bar at Lola's at Century House in Vancouver—a city that has recently become a hot party destination for Hollywood celebrities—is Lola. (It is her restaurant after all.) She got her first job behind the stick in the late 1970s and joined the staff at Delilah's in Vancouver about six years later. It's a fanciful establishment with a viciously opulent decor that's dedicated to feeding its patrons an array of victuals between their tasting rounds of the massive Martini menu. Delilah's had twelve varieties when Lola arrived, but by the time she left to open Lola's at Century House in 1995, the list had grown to nearly sixty variations—many of them invented by Lola herself.

"When we opened Lola's at Century House, Marion [her partner and another former Delilah's bartender] and I knew that we had to create our own Martini and champagne cocktail list." Once again, the pair created an avant repertoire of gin- and vodka-based Martinis (passion fruit, raspberry, cranberry, for example) which they present in individual shakers accompanied by frosty cocktail glasses. (Sorry, you won't find a brandy- or tequila-based Martini at this establishment.)

Professional female mixologists, like Lola and Marion, have come into their own in the last decade of the twentieth century. As Lola herself casually comments: "Women are super-tasters. It's in their makeup to be more orally sensitive to tastes and textures. They can detect subtle differences." That talent has certainly earned both Lola and Marion a place in the Martini Mixologists' Hall of Fame. Lola agrees that the Martini renaissance harkens back to the days when baby-boomers were teenagers who were told that "you can't do this or that. The kids are doing that again."

The Lola can also be served as a dinner finale. Lola's serves a **Lola Granitée**. Combine all the ingredients in a glass or metal bowl and place it in the freezer hours ahead of time. Every twenty minutes or so, use a fork to break up and stir any ice that forms. Do it quickly and put it right back in the freezer so it doesn't melt. You should end up with a sorbet consistency. When it's all frozen, you don't have to stir it any more, and it'll keep for a few days. If it doesn't freeze at all, try again using less alcohol and more juice.

MANDARIN MARTINI

CREATED BY OLIVER'S AT THE MAYFLOWER PARK HOTEL

Shake

1.5 oz. (45 ml)
Stolichnaya Vodka

0.5 oz. (15 ml)
Bombay Sapphire Gin

1 splash
Mandarin Napoleon
Liqueur

1 dash
Cointreau

mandarin orange slice

mandarin orange twist

Pour the liqueur into a glass shaker. Swirl to coat and drain. Fill the shaker with ice. Build the remaining ingredients, including the orange slice, over the ice and shake. Place garnish in a chilled glass and pour.

One popular combination we've seen ordered in the hot Martini lounges pays homage to the 1930s Orange Blossom—a 2:1 blend of gin and orange juice—and the Screwdriver, the long drink of choice at many 1970s Sunday brunches. People's taste in food and drink has become more daring and refined over the years. So more elegant elements have been used to introduce a subtle orange fragrance. One of the best examples, the Mandarin Martini, won the award for Best Specialty Martini at the 1995 Seattle Martini Competition.

Oliver's also serves **L'Orangerie**, rinsing the ice with 1 splash Grand Marnier, shaking 2 oz. (60 ml) Tanqueray Sterling Vodka, and topping it with an orange twist garnish.

The **Orange Magnet** at Set 'Em Up Joe blends 3 oz. (90 ml) Bombay Sapphire Gin, 0.5 oz. (15 ml) Cointreau, and an orange slice garnish.

The **Northwest Sunset** made at the Garden Court at the Four Seasons Olympic blends with 2 oz. (60 ml) Ketel One Vodka, 0.5 oz. (15 ml) Canton Ginger Liqueur, and 1 splash orange juice.

The **Elegant** at Set 'Em Up Joe combines 3 oz. (90 ml) Tanqueray Sterling Vodka with 1 splash Grand Marnier.

We've also made an **Orange Flower**—2 oz. (60 ml) Stolichnaya Vodka, 0.5 oz. (15 ml) Curaçao, and 2 drops orange flower water—and a **Noonday Sun** which replaces the water with dashes of freshly-squeezed orange and lemon juices.

GLACIER BLUE

CREATED BY GARDEN COURT AT THE FOUR SEASONS OLYMPIC

Blue drinks are a hot item in many swanky lounges. But like blue-tinted food, not everyone appreciates the finer points of a cocktail that looks like someone unloaded a fountain pen into the glass. In John Mitchell's comic novel–*Very Vicky and the Secret of the Bronx Cocktail*–Vicky's acquaintance, Brooksie, shrieks when she hears that blue Martinis are part of a Nazi plot: "A blue Martini sounds like a horror, darlings, a simple horror! Trust aged Axis lackeys to harness a Martini for evil!"

Nevertheless, the Glacier Blue did win the 1992 Seattle Martini Competition's Specialty Martini Award, and lounge lizards love them. Just make sure you're color coordinated for the night–wear chartreuse, fuschia, or tangerine–or opt for a leopard-skin print which goes with just about everything.

Shake

2 oz. (60 ml) Stolichnaya Gold Vodka

1 oz. (30 ml) Bombay Sapphire Gin

0.5 oz. (15 ml) Blue Curaçao

orange slice or a few fresh nasturtium petals (See fresh and preserved petal garnish instructions on page 101).

One [Martini] is alright, two is too many, and three is not enough.
—James Thurber

The **Chicago Blue** at Set 'Em Up Joe mixes 3 oz. (90 ml) Tanqueray Sterling Vodka and 0.5 oz. (15 ml) Blue Curaçao.

The Blue Lizard Lounge's **Blue Lizard Martini** shakes 2 oz (60 ml) vodka and 1 drop Blue Curaçao.

A **Blue Monday** shakes up 2 oz (60 ml) vodka, 0.5 oz. (15 ml) Blue Curaçao, and 0.5 oz. (15 ml) Cointreau.

COSMOPOLITAN

CREATED BY LOLA OF LOLA'S AT CENTURY HOUSE

Although Martinis are definitely unisex cocktails, the Cosmopolitan seems to be a more feminine favorite. Yes it's got color, it's got taste. But we have another reason for you to like this particular cocktail. When Cape Cods and Madras were stylish in the 1980s, our bartender at Mary Lou's in Manhattan told us that the blend of alcohol and cranberry juice was a good way to keep healthy after those all-nighters that started somewhere in Tribeca and somehow ended in the West Village. The Cosmopolitan and its variants allow you to sip this rejuvenating combo in style.

Let stand

2 oz. (60 ml)
Stolichnaya Vodka

I splash
cranberry juice cocktail

I dash of each:
Rose's Lime Cordial and
Cointreau

lemon twist

Don't make this drink with super-strength cranberry juice from the natural food store. Your cheeks will disappear into your teeth from the tartness.

They say that a Martini is like a woman's breast. One ain't enough and three is too many.
    —Gayle the cocktail waitress, *Parallax View*

Lola's **Metropolitan** blends 2 oz. (60 ml) Bombay Gin, splashes of cranberry juice cocktail and margarita mix, a squeeze of fresh lemon juice, and six fresh cranberries for garnish. Her **Seabreeze** replaces the margarita mix with grapefruit juice.

Our **Perfect Cosmopolitan** blends 1.5 oz. (45 ml) Stolichnaya Gold Vodka, 0.75 oz. (22.5 ml) Cointreau, I dash Rose's Lime Cordial, I splash cranberry juice cocktail, and a squeeze of lemon juice.

The **Montini**—signature drink at the Monterey Grill—adds I splash crème de cassis. Their **Sunset Martini** blends 2 oz. (60 ml) Bombay Sapphire Gin with splashes of Rose's Lime Cordial and cranberry juice cocktail.

The Chateau Marmot's Bar Marmot makes their **Cosmopolitan** using 3.5 oz. (105 ml) infused vodka (see *Instilled Essences* on page 154), 0.5 oz. (15 ml) Triple Sec, I splash Rose's Lime Cordial, and a maraschino cherry garnish.

MIDORI MARTINI
CREATED BY SUNTORY, LIMITED

When a friend sent us a bottle of Midori Liqueur, we'd never heard of it before. Unfortunately, it didn't come with instructions. And while we instinctively made a fabulous drink (which we later found out is called a Melon Ball), we weren't too sure what else to do with it. Then one summer evening, at cocktail time, we discovered that we were out of anything that closely resembled vermouth. At that moment, our forgotten bottle of Midori seemed to leap to the fore, like an eager volunteer ready to face the odds. One sip and we were convinced that green isn't just for St. Patrick's Day.

Shake

1.5 oz. (45 ml)
Beefeater Gin

0.5 oz. (15 ml)
Gancia Dry Vermouth

1 splash
Suntory Midori Liqueur

a red plum (aka: *ume*)

Lola's own version—**Friend of Dorothy**—blends 2 oz. (60 ml) Stolichnaya Vodka and splashes of Suntory Midori Liqueur and Rose's Lime Cordial.

Our own **Melon Ball** mixes 2 oz. (60 ml) Stolichnaya Vodka and splashes each of both Suntory Midori Liqueur and fresh orange juice.

When the shadow of the grasshopper falls across the trail of the field mouse on the green and slimy grass as a red sun rises above the western horizon silhouetting a gaunt and tautly muscled Indian warrior perched with bow and arrow cocked and aimed straight at you it's time for another Martini.
—An anonymous passage written on the mural outside Vesuvio's Café in San Francisco, CA

Let stand

2 oz. (60 ml)
Moskovskaya Vodka

0.5 oz. (15 ml) of each:
Malibu Coconut Rum and
Triple Sec

2 drops
Angostura Bitters

lime twist

**LESSON ONE:
HANGOVER
PREVENTATIVES**
Ever been told that you
should eat bread or pasta
because it'll soak up the alcohol? Or perhaps the advice
was to consume fat, it'll coat
your stomach and prevent
undue absorption. (Isn't that
silly?) One journalist drank a
cup of olive oil before a
night out. We're sure it kept
his coat shiny (that's what
our cat's vet says), but even
if it did work, personally
we'd settle for a hangover.
Truth is, any food slows
down alcohol absorption in
your system, but nothing
stops it.

Hair of the arachnid that bit you?
Hunting for a Martini in a land of umbrella drinks? Wonder what Martini
drinkers do on vacation? Here's one
couple's adventure:

While vacationing in Hawaii and
staying at the Four Seasons, my husband had a Martini experience. He
got out of the shower one morning
and noticed a red dime-sized spot on
his wrist. I proceeded to tell him that
a woman had gotten bitten by a
brown spider while vacuuming, lapsed
into a coma, and, by the time they
found her they had to cut off both her
arms and her legs! This didn't cheer
him up. We stopped at the concierge
to show him...and he let us know that
in Hawaii they take bites very seriously.

Despite that we went out and had
a late night *full* of Martinis. We
stopped at the lobby bar for a "final
final" one and met a couple on their
honeymoon. We showed the bartender the bite, and the couple had
also heard the story about the woman
and the brown spider. They offered
to buy John his "final" drink. We all
had a good laugh.

We went to bed (or maybe passed
out), but around 12:30 A.M. I was
awakened by a knock at the door....I
ignored it because, who did I know
in Maui? The knocking came again.
I knew that my husband...way on the
other side of the king size bed would
never hear it, so I got up.

I first peered through the keyhole,
then opened the door and found my
husband stark naked in the hallway.
My first response was, "Where have

you been?" He was not amused. He seemed to have walked in his sleep…which he had never done before…and awoke just in time to watch the door lock shut!! Now he was naked in the hallway of a five-star hotel!! Luckily, I woke up and let him in. It has been great fun over and over in the retelling!!!

Was it the bite or the Martinis? We'll probably never know!

Tropical twists can spell the end of a serious cocktail (just try to look cosmopolitan clutching a big frosty Piña Colada). You'll be happy to know that among the hundreds of Martini recipes we've encountered (and the hundreds more that–even by the most liberal standards and despite being served in a Martini glass–aren't Martinis), we haven't uncovered a single one that includes a cocktail umbrella. Though maybe that little parasol is just the thing for the extra-dry Martini lover–to ward off excess humidity and protect the drink from dilution by sudden thunderstorms.

Lola's **Patricia Delicia** combines 2 oz. (60 ml) Stolichnaya Vodka, splashes of passionfruit juice and papaya juice, and a lime slice garnish.

The **Tropical Dream** at Set 'Em Up Joe combines 3 oz. (90 ml) Fris Vodka, 1 oz. (30 ml) Malibu Coconut Rum, and 1 splash pineapple juice.

Its 1930s predecessor, the **Miami Special**, shook up equal parts gin and pineapple juice, 1 splash French vermouth, and 2 dashes Curaçao.

Another tropical concoction–a **Banana Martini**–made at the Monkey Bar in New York, shakes up 2.5 oz. (75 ml) Skyy Vodka, splashes of crème de banane and Martini & Rossi Extra-Dry Vermouth, and a carmelized banana slice garnish.

I think we just made an important medical discovery. If you act drunk long enough, you can get a hangover.
—Hawkeye Pierce, M*A*S*H

FORTUNELLA

CREATED BY OLIVER'S AT THE MAYFLOWER PARK HOTEL

Shake

1 oz. (30 ml)
Ketel One Vodka

0.75 oz. (22.5 ml)
of each:
Bombay Sapphire Gin and
Caravella

1 splash of each:
Campari and Cointreau

1 tsp.
candied kumquat nectar

lemon slice

lemon twist and a
kumquat

Coat a chilled shaker with Campari and drain. Fill with ice and add remaining ingredients. Shake, strain, and garnish.

So there we were at 3 A.M., crossing the border from Washington state into British Columbia after sampling our eighth and last Martini–the "lucky"Fortunella–at the 1996 Seattle Martini Competition. (It's an innocent, fruity drink that made the perfect "dessert" after an evening of Martini-tasting.) The customs officer waived us through without a second look. Guess she recognized us, or maybe it was just because she couldn't wait to see what the police at the roadblock a hundred yards further would make of a couple in full formal evening dress heading north with a pile of party Polaroids scattered across the back seat.

"Great outfits!" the officer remarked as she flashed her light across us and then the photos, "Just get married?"

"No," I replied, glancing furtively at the line of cars they'd already impounded that night, "we were just at the Seattle Martini Competition."

She didn't even need to ask. She just raised an eyebrow, "And?"

"A sip, hours before I got behind the wheel. No more. She," I gestured toward Anistatia (who was struggling to suppress a fit of laughter), "got to be designated drinker for the night."

I was waiting for her to order us out of the car when she waved us through. A thought went through my mind as we breezed past the line-up of cars that didn't clear the roadblock waiting to be searched. Maybe there is a sweet bit of luck to be had from drinking a Fortunella.

WILLIAM TELL

CREATED BY LOLA OF LOLA'S AT THE CENTURY HOUSE

Ah, first they thought it was just red wine, and maybe beer. Finally the medical profession at large have recognized the health benefits of any alcoholic beverage consumed in moderation (which means opting for less at present in favor of having more of a future).

With that generic comment in mind, you really could say that an apple Martini like the William Tell or the Palace Apple Skyy a day keeps the doctor away. (Although when it comes to fun, three or four are sometimes more–fun that is.) As one anonymous drinker put it, "He who has but one drink a day, lives to die some other way."

Let stand

2 oz. (60 ml) Stolichnaya Vodka

I splash of each: apple juice and Rose's Lime Cordial

lime slice

The Palace Kitchen makes a **Palace Apple Skyy** using 1.5 oz. (45 ml) Skyy Vodka, 0.5 oz. (15 ml) Bizouard Calvados, 2 drops Goldschlager, and a grilled apple garnish.

Adapted from *Playboy's Host & Bar Book*, the **Saint-Lô** mixes 2 oz. (60 ml) Stolichnaya Vodka, 0.5 oz. (15 ml) Calvados, and I splash lemon juice.

Our own version, the **Apple Pie**, combines 2 oz. (60 ml) Stoli® Zinamon Vodka and I splash Calvados, garnished with a cinnamon stick or a lemon twist.

LESSON TWO: HANGOVER PREVENTATIVES

There are a few things you can do before you go to sleep (or pass out). Take two aspirin and drink a pint or two of orange juice. One probable cause of post-Bacchanalian distress is a constriction of blood vessels in the brain; aspirin is a mild vaso-dialator. One other problem stems from severe dehydration. Alcohol actually sucks liquid out of your system, orange juice replenishes it.

Take a multivitamin. It's rumored that vitamin-B depletion contributes to the brain damage found in career drinkers.

MARTINI NAVRATILOVA

CREATED BY LOLA OF LOLA'S AT CENTURY HOUSE

Let stand

**2 oz. (60 ml)
Stolichnaya Vodka**

**1 splash
Gatorade**

lemon slice

*Take the hair, it is well
written,
Of the dog by which
you're bitten
Work off one wine by his
brother
One labor with another.*
—Antiphanes, 473 B.C.

Eggs Benedict was
invented in 1894 by
Lemuel Benedict, a
patron at the Waldorf-
Astoria Hotel. Hungover
and desperate for a
cure, he ordered
poached eggs over ham
on buttered toast
topped with Hollandaise
sauce. The maître d'hôtel
was so impressed, he
named the dish after Mr.
Benedict.

"I don't see why more people order
the Friend of Dorothy (*see page 93*) than
they do the Martini Navratilova," Lola
casually remarked. "The Gatorade is actually much better. It replaces the electrolytes you lose when you drink so you
don't get a hangover."

Electrolytes, for those of you who slept
through high-school chemistry and
didn't bother to take it again in college,
are salts. They aren't the sodium chlo-
ride you find on pretzels, they're other
salts that your body needs. You've seen
how well they work for athletes like tennis champ Martina Navratilova and
the Boston Marathon runners, so it
must have some value for competitors
in the Party-Night Olympics. Besides,
a green-tinted drink could keep you
from looking as green as Jared did one
fateful morning after:

> I was sitting in the Empire Diner
> at 11A.M. (a very unchic hour to be
> there), gripping the edge of the table
> though it didn't slow the pace of the
> room's rotation. I guess the waitress
> knew the signs of a bender's revenge
> (all I did was ask her to pour the wa-
> ter a little more quietly), because she
> gave me a matronly smile and boomed,
> "Hangover, eh?"
>
> "No," I replied, rolling a jaun-
> diced eye skyward from the menu
> that I was (by this time) lying face
> down on. "The green complexion is
> from the lizard side of my family."

Somehow, the Lava Lamp–one of the supreme symbols of 1970s hip (right up there with water beds and shag carpets)–has survived. We spent the better part of one afternoon sitting in a seriously swank 70s-style lounge not too long ago. They were playing everything from early Parliament Funkadelic to the *I Dream of Jeannie* theme song. The conversation shifted to fake-fur-covered beanbag chairs, streaking, the Hustle, eight track tapes, platform shoes, polyester, Kiss, *Charlie's Angels*, and everything else that's been gone long enough to become nostalgic memorabilia. A lava lamp behind the bar grabbed our attention, and after a while we started to wonder if we could get a Martini to do that.

Back home it was trial and error. But finally we hit on a combination that produced those same mellow undulations in the bottom of a cocktail glass. Obviously, this is not a serious Martini, but then again, there are times when life isn't meant to be taken that seriously. This is just the drink for those times.

Shake

3 oz. (90 ml)
Stolichnaya Vodka

I splash of each:
Chambord (raspberry liqueur) and honey

Blend the Chambord and honey in a shot glass with a spoon. Shake the vodka on ice and strain it into a glass, then spoon in the Chambord mix.

An **Orange Lava Lamp** replaces the Chambord with 4 drops Angostura Bitters.

The **Black Martini** is simpler to make. Shake the vodka and Chambord, and eliminate the honey.

The Loring Café in Minneapolis makes a **Captain Lambchop**: 2 oz. (60 ml) vodka, I oz. (30 ml) sweet and sour cocktail mix, 0.5 oz. (15 ml)

LESSON THREE: HANGOVER PALLIATIVES

First let's clear something up about the adage, "Haf a lil' hair of th' dog that bit'cha." More alcohol on the morning after doesn't cure a hangover. It does postpone the inevitable (we've met a few people who've been staving off theirs for years, and believe us it's not pretty), but you'll have to face it eventually, and dog hair will make it much worse in the end.

If you're feeling brave, try the wives' tale remedies: sniffing a little mentholated rub; drinking a Prairie Oyster (Worcestershire, lemon juice, a raw egg, and a splash of vodka); or drinking an Eye Opener (a raw egg and lemon juice in a shot of whisky or gin).

Take a hot shower, sauna, or a steambath. Get rid of those puffy bags under your eyes: Take a tablespoon and submerge it in a glassful of ice water for about a minute. Then close your eye and cup the chilled spoon gently over the lid.

If you can resist eating much of anything for a few hours and concentrate on rehydrating, when you do eat it should mark the end of your hangover.

Chambord, dashes of Cointreau, Grand Marnier, Rose's Lime Cordial, and 3 lime slices for garnish.

The Naked Lunch in New York creates a **Red Skyy**, mixing 1 oz. (30 ml) Skyy Vodka, 1 jigger raspberry-white grape juice, and a blackberry garnish. Rinse the glass with Martini & Rossi Sweet Vermouth and dip the rim in red sugar (available in the baking section of most grocery stores).

If you want to try another purple Martini, make a **Jack Horner**: 2 oz. (60 ml) Stolichnaya Vodka, splashes of Sljivovica Old Plum Brandy or Slijivowicz, fresh orange juice, fresh lemon juice, and a brandied cherry garnish.

The ultimate purple Martini, however, is definitely the **Purple Haze**: 2 oz. (60 ml) Stolichnaya Vodka with splashes of both Blue Curaçao and cranberry juice cocktail to give it color. It lives up to the Jimi Hendrix song it's named after.

If that doesn't satisfy those retro urges, Patrick Gerding created a **Gilligan's Island**: 2 oz. (60 ml) Absolut Vodka and splashes of both pineapple juice and Grand Marnier, garnished with lime twists. Now if Gilligan isn't your type, you might prefer Ginger (*see Wild Ginger on page 117*).

FLOWERS & CHOCOLATES
DESSERT MARTINIS

Flowers, chocolates, enticing cocktails: these are the essences of romance. A recent magazine survey asked its readers: "Is chocolate better than sex?" We say, why choose one or the other! Chocolate Martinis are a little of both, blended, and served chilled.

Why make a chocolate Martini, when there are other cocoa-based drinks out there? Because they're rich without being sugary, they have the relaxing effect of a classic Martini, and when you first try them, they're an incredible surprise.

Flowers as garnish can make a real statement: whether you're celebrating the Rites of Spring, or just announcing the severity of your mid-winter cabin fever. And if the night calls for sheets scattered with rose petals, there's nothing like a few matching Martinis to set the mood.

If you've never munched on flower petals, they're not pungent or sweet. In fact, most of the edible varieties have a tangy edge that's perfect in a Martini. Rose petals, for example, have a surprisingly dry flavor and have only the faintest scent of rose to them.

I'm angry. Somebody slipped a brown Martini in on me. Perhaps it's that sappy bartender using mascara again.
— Ernie Kovacs
(as Percy Dovetonsil)

PRESERVED PETALS

If you want to garnish your drink with flowers or petals, make sure they're pesticide-free. Some high-end grocery stores farmers' markets sell edible flowers. Nasturtiums are pretty good; so are roses, violets, and daisies (avoid the bitter yellow centers). They can be used fresh or preserved.

To preserve petals for garnish, cover the bottom of a small bowl with sugar. Place the petals on the sugar so they're not touching each other. Cover them with more sugar and let them sit for a few days in a cool, dry place. To make sugar encrusted "candied" petals, brush them with a little pasteurized egg white.

For a savory garnish, try the Japanese approach: bury each flower in salt on a plate, and press them with another plate on top for a day. Rinse petals briefly under hot water before use.

PERCY DOVETONSIL

INSPIRED BY AN ERNIE KOVACS CHARACTER

Shake

2 oz. (60 ml)
Bombay Sapphire Gin

1 splash
Kina Lillet Blanc

1 dash
Curaçao

a fresh daisy with
a stuffed green olive
skewered on the end
of the stem (cut the stem
to about 3" in length)

(See fresh and preserved
flower petal garnish in-
structions on page 101.)

I complained about the daisy [in my Martini] being unreal the other day. [Now] they have a real daisy in here, real gin in here, and a real stuffed olive. Only the pimento is plastic.

—Ernie Kovacs
(as Percy Dovetonsil)

"Greetings from your orthocon tube," Percy Dovetonsil chimed at the opening of the *Ernie Kovacs Show* during the late 1950s and early 1960s. Wearing a tiger-skin print satin smoking jacket with black velvet lapels and cuffs–accessorized with a silk ascot–and sipping a Martini garnished with an olive attached to a fresh daisy, Dovetonsil was an inspiration for modern-day lounge lizards.

Most baby-boomers discovered the euphoric effects of Martinis while observing their parents at cocktail parties. I confess Ernie Kovacs and his weekly television broadcasts raised my curiosity about the potent potable. Kovacs' self-proclaimed poet laureate opened his segment by taking a sip, nibbling the olive, and making a simple comment like: "Actually, these Martinis that I drink are particularly wonderful because there's a very attractive young lady here in the studio who dips her little finger in it each time. Too bad she doesn't trim her nails."

Other times, his salutation would be a little more involved:

Greetings. Greetings indeed. There has been some talk that I'm drinking real gin in this glass for my Martini. I objurgate such talk. It's not gin. It's a phony prop. It's white scotch. Besides, last week I had to join AA to continue in this spot. I did. It's Albert Alexander's bar. It's a wonderful little place.

Seeing this happy tippler sitting on a swing, playing a piano, or reciting one of his immortal odes to bookworms, fad diets, or other inconsequential anomalies (that went right over my pre-adolescent head) while sipping a Martini, was probably the biggest influence on my adult drinking habits. The cigar-smoking Kovacs also elevated my appreciation of music, playing excerpts from Kurt Weill's *Three-Penny Opera* and Juan Garcia Esquivel hits like *Sentimental Journey* and *Mucha Muchacha*.

A few years later, Kovacs and Dovetonsil were no more. They were quickly replaced by an undying infatuation with Sean Connery and his super spy character, James Bond. It took a few decades of Martini consumption before I learned the comprehensive subtlety one can achieve from sipping the elixir: while watching a Kovacs retrospective, I *finally* noticed that Whistler's mother was riding a Harley in the painting behind Percy Dovetonsil!

I digress. As Dovetonsil commented in the last show: "I think I know where that extra bottle of Martinis went that I had here, it's up in the control room."

The **Fawlty Flower** made at Delilah's mixes 2 oz. (60 ml) vodka and 1 splash fresh lime juice. Preserved flower petals are floated on top.

Our own invention—the **American Beauty** —blends 2 oz. (60 ml) Bombay Sapphire Gin with splashes of Bols Apricot Brandy and Cinzano Dry Vermouth and 1 dash grenadine. The rosy mixture is then garnished with a fresh red rose petal.

(See fresh and preserved flower petal garnish instructions on page 101.)

THE 911

Let stand

2 oz. (60 ml)
Stolichnaya Gold Vodka

1 splash of each:
Godiva Chocolate Liqueur
and fresh raspberry purée

fresh raspberry

The **Chocotini** served
at Ken Stewart's Grille
mixes 2 oz. (60 ml)
Stolichnaya Vodka and 1
oz. (30 ml) white crème
de cacao, garnished with a
thoroughly washed, whole,
fresh strawberry.

You've all heard the plaintive cry of a chocoholic in mid-afternoon withdrawal crying, "I need an emergency chocolate fix." You've watched them salivate at the sight of a giant Toblerone bar; experience orgasmic satisfaction as they consume the first bite of a handrolled chocolate truffle. Well, some of these wanton souls are also Martini drinkers. We really hadn't experienced the addictive nature of a chocolate Martini until we dined one evening at Lola's and stimulated our appetites with The 911. Then we understood. We got around to ordering duck confit and perfectly grilled lamb chops a few drinks later.

Purists might feel that a chocolate Martini chilled in the very shaker that caresses their classic blend is sacrilegious. But chocolate–like Martinis, music, and memorable romantic companions–is a seductively sensual treat. So why not combine two lovely vices in a shaker while listening to the third, and eventually sharing it with a fourth?

TOOTSIE ROLL MARTINI

CREATED BY JERRY LANGLAND

One midwesterner we know, Jerry Langland, is a chocolate Martini connoisseur. He's tried every variation that can be found within the Chicagoland area. That's not an easy feat. When we recently visited the Windy City, we discovered that the home of Vienna Red Hot wieners, thick-crust Sicilian pizzas, and foot-long racks of barbecued ribs is also chocolate Martini lover's heaven. (Maybe it's the aroma of Milk Duds wafting from the Holloway Candy Company production plant near the downtown area that's inspired everyone to order chocolate-laced drinks.)

Jerry's favorite, the Tootsie Roll Martini, harkens back to another childhood treat: Tootsie Rolls and Tootsie Pops. The love affair doesn't end there. For every scrumptious cocoa-based candy or pastry you can imagine, Langland's shaken up a liquid version to appease his all-consuming passion.

Chicago is also famous (or is it notorious) for its wealth of bars, lounges, and nightclubs as well as its more-than-generous double-sized drinks, served in birdbath-sized cocktail glasses, and 4 A.M. closing times. With odds like that, it was impossible to run out of watering holes (and avoid massive consumption) as we searched for liquid confections. As the winter winds whipped through the streets, we kept warm on a diet of luscious Martinis served in cocoa-powder-rimmed cocktail glasses, garnished with Hershey's Chocolate Kisses, and laced with fruit or nut fla-

Shake

2 oz. (60 ml) of each:
Stolichnaya Gold Vodka
and Godiva Chocolate
Liqueur

0.5 oz. (15 ml)
Grand Marnier

orange slice

Cointreau can also be used in place of Grand Marnier if you want a stronger orange essence.

Our own **Chocolate Blossom** mixes 2 oz. (60 ml) Stolichnaya Vodka, 1 splash Godiva Chocolate Liqueur, and 1 dash Triple Sec, garnished with a fresh nasturtium. (See fresh and preserved flower petal garnishes on page 101.)

So what do you serve with a chocolate Martini? Try a plate of strawberries with the tops trimmed off, surrounding a dish of Godiva chocolates. To brighten the flavor of the berries, stand them cut side down in a tablespoon or two of balsamic vinegar. (If you're skeptical, try it on a single berry first. We served them that way to the general manager of a luxury hotel. His reaction: "Where'd you find such perfect strawberries at this time of year?")

vors reminiscent of a Valentine's Day candy sampler.

To say the least, when we left Chicago our cravings for Tootsie Rolls and anything else made with chocolate were totally satisfied.

According to Langland, the variations on this theme are endless. Try other tastes like Amaretto di Saronno, Frangelico, or Chambord.

Langland's **Double Chocolate Martini** blends equal parts Stolichnaya Vodka, Godiva Chocolate Liqueur, and Kahlua or Baileys Irish Cream.

His **Mixed Chocolate/Chocolate Swirl** blends equal parts Stolichnaya Vodka, Godiva Chocolate Liqueur, and Godet White Chocolate Liqueur.

Set 'Em Up Joe's **Chocolate Kiss** combines 3 oz. (90 ml) Tanqueray Sterling Vodka, 0.5 oz. (15 ml) Bols Dark Crème de Cacao, 1 dash heavy cream, and a Hershey's Chocolate Kiss garnish.

The Jet Lounge in Manhattan makes a **Chocolate-Tini** blending 1 jigger Ketel One Vodka, 0.5 oz. (15 ml) clear crème de cacao, 1 splash Martini & Rossi Dry Vermouth, and a Hershey's Chocolate Kiss garnish.

SAKURATINI

CREATED BY SUNTORY, LIMITED

Sipping Sakuratinis in Tokyo during cherry blossom season reminded us of an art that Japan introduced to the West over five centuries ago: flower arrangement. The Japanese have no equivalent for the word "love." However, they do convey that emotion without words by sending their loved ones specific flowers arranged to convey various messages. (They even created the perfect floral "Dear John" letter: a single yellow rose sent with a mirror and a comb which loosely means "I no longer see you behind me in the morning as I comb my hair because I have lost my love for you.")

In the West, the language of flowers is described in books like *The People's Almanac* by Irving Wallace and *Webster's New Collegiate Dictionary*. There are even a few edible varieties that have hidden meanings like nasturtiums, peach blossoms, apple blossoms, jasmine, bachelor buttons, rosemary, cherry blossoms, chrysanthemums, pansies, orange blossoms, sunflowers, clover, marigolds, zinnias, roses, and violets. Garnish your date's Martini with a secret floral message! You could say a lot over a couple of drinks without ever uttering a word.

Shake

3 oz. (90 ml)
Suntory Reserve Whisky
or Bombay Sapphire Gin

1 oz. (30 ml)
Suntory Sakura Liqueur
(cherry liqueur)

preserved cherry blossom
(See fresh and preserved
flower petal garnish
instructions on page 101.)

SAY IT WITH FLOWERS
We found a few edible floral garnishes that express hidden thoughts of love:

APPLE BLOSSOM:
"I prefer you."

CHRYSANTHEMUM:
(red): "I love you"; (other colors) "I feel slighted."

DAISY:
(white) "You are innocent."

PEACH BLOSSOM:
"I am your captive."

ROSE:
(deep red) "I am bashful"; (white) "I am worthy of you"; (yellow) "I don't love you."

VIOLET:
(blue) "I'm faithful to you."

Lola's **Ma Chérie** mixes 2 oz. (60 ml) vodka infused with sun dried cherries and 1 splash cherry brandy. (See *Instilled Essences* on page 154.)

THE SILK ROAD
SPICE AND CAJUN MARTINIS

The secret to longevity? Never travel to any place you haven't been before, never stay up past 8 P.M., always go to bed alone, and never drink another Martini. Follow these simple rules and you still may not live forever, but it'll sure seem like forever.

Every time we sip a cinnamon-laced Martini, we remember when we were kids combing the issues of *National Geographic*. Those dreams of exotic destinations dance through our heads once again. Did you ever want to retrace the Spice Route that snaked northward from Ivory Coast to the Casbah? Did you ever want to traverse the Silk Road, trading tea from the Far East in exchange for European almonds and other delights? Did you ever want to brave the American frontier like Jack London's spicy characters who sought their fortunes in gold instead of cinnamon or pepper?

Then have another sip of an icy-hot Cajun Martini and we'll meet you on the bayou, *chèr*.

THE MOROCCAN ODYSSEY

INSPIRED BY GERALD POSNER

The legendary African and Asian Spice Routes yielded more than a wealth of cinnamon, nutmeg, licorice, and pepper. Many of these exotic spices were bound for European gin and vermouth distillers who added the precious ingredients to their secret formulations. The road to Timbuktu also appropriately serves as the backdrop for a fabulous modern-day adventure, recounted for us by author and journalist Gerald Posner:

Several years ago my wife, Trisha, and I visited Marrakesh, and after a few days decided to venture south over the Atlas Mountains toward the edge of the Sahara desert. After a couple of days of travel, and spending nights in centuries-old kasbahs along the way, we reached the outpost of Zagora. It was there that the paved road ended and the Sahara started in earnest (our journey ended there). At the edge of Zagora is a sign posted in both Arabic and French, announcing "52 DAYS BY CAMEL TO TIMBUKTU."

A few blocks away from that intimidating notice is a café/coffee shop run by a slightly disheveled Bedouin. It was nearly sunset when we made our way into his shop, empty except for a couple of Arab men in the corner sipping mint tea. My wife and I needed a pick-me-up.

"Coffee?" No.

"Cold water." No.

We declined the owner's offer of mint tea, having had enough in the last week to last a lifetime. "Lemonade," my

Shake

2 oz. (60 ml)
Bombay Gin

0.5 oz. (15 ml)
dry sherry

1 pinch
nutmeg or cinnamon

If you can find it, try Paarl Oloroso: a dry sherry imported from South Africa.

Here are a few appropriate toasts if you're traveling to Africa or the Middle East:
- Egypt: Fee sihetak!
- Tanzania: Kwa afya yako!
- Israel: L'Chayim!

The **Goldfinger** served at Lola's, blends 2 oz. (60 ml) Stolichnaya Gold Vodka and 1 splash Goldschlager. If you're feeling rich, crumple a sheet of gold leaf into the glass for the garnish.

Lola's **Gotham** mixes 2 oz. (60 ml) Stolichnaya Vodka and 1 splash Luxardo Sambuca Passione Nera.

SPICE LIQUEURS AND CORDIALS

CARAWAY:
kümmel, Akavit

CINNAMON:
Goldschlager

COFFEE:
Kahlua, Tia Maria

GINGER:
Canton Ginger Liqueur

HERB AND SPICES:
Benedictine, Chartreuse, Yellow Chartreuse, Jägermeister, Galliano, Tuaca, Strega

LICORICE:
Luxardo Sambuca Passione Nera, absinthe, Pernod, Ouzo

NUTS:
Amaretto (almond), Frangelico (hazelnut), Nocello (walnut)

PEPPERMINT:
peppermint schnapps

wife took a wild stab. Just a grunt and shake of the head.

We were ready to leave when Trisha almost mumbled to me, "What I would really like is an icy Martini."

"Martini?" It was as though the Bedouin had suddenly received a slight electrical jolt. He popped up from behind his wooden counter, reached into a corner behind a sink, and to our astonishment proudly displayed a classic Martini glass. A big smile crossed his face at our puzzlement.

We looked at each other and almost simultaneously moved back to grab two chairs at a table. The whole purpose of this journey was adventure, so how could we be foolish enough to walk away from this. To this day, we are not quite sure what ingredients our "bartender" mixed, but it was definitely a heavy dose of gin (that, judging by its roughness, must have been aging in the Saharan sun for some time) and I thought there was some white wine added, although Trisha tasted sherry (she's British, so may have a natural inclination to sherry that should probably be discounted!). An olive, stuffed with an anchovy was plopped into each glass (don't try that one yourself). Everything was served at room temperature, but considering the alternative of mint tea, it was a particularly wonderful Martini. It was far from the best Martini we have ever had, but we don't remember one that was timed better or more appreciated. One though was definitely enough, as we figured it was after three or four of these that tourists inevitably decided the fifty-two days by camel to Timbuktu sounded reasonable.

COPENHAGEN

ADAPTED FROM A RECIPE BY KINGSLEY AMIS

An old friend from Denmark came for a visit recently. When we offered him a cocktail, he said, "In my country we always drink until the liquor cabinet's empty." We'd just bought a couple of bottles of vodka and a bottle of Akavit, and let him open the cabinet figuring he'd be eating those words when he saw the amount of booze in it. He pulled open the cupboard, stepped back...and grinned. We knew it was going to be a long night.

As he began shaking the first round of double-strength, high-potency Copenhagens, we realized our fears were well-founded. In a last-ditch effort to avert excruciating hangovers (and to give us a snowball's chance of clearing out the whole cabinet), we invited everyone we could get on the phone. Unfortunately, every time we got someone on the line, he'd shout out in the background, "Tell 'em to bring more booze." Good thing we'd stocked up on almonds before he arrived.

Shake

2 oz. (60 ml) Smirnoff Vodka

0.5 oz. (15 ml) Akavit

blanched almonds

Kingsley Amis believed that the almond was placed in this drink as a Nordic good-luck token that "will keep your guests' tongues wagging until the liquor sets them wagging about anything under the sun."

For those of you who've never encountered "Scandinavian courage" (aka: Akavit), it's a clear liquid that looks, pours, and is served like a another Nordic favorite—vodka. However, Akavit's taste has a lot more in common with a loaf of rye bread than with winter wheat. That's right, it's distilled with caraway seeds just like its liqueur cousin kümmel.

Another unique spiced Martini is flavored with cardamom. The Raincity Grill pours a **Spicy Rose** made with 3 oz. (90 ml) vodka infused with green cardamom seeds and 1 splash rose water. (See *Instilled Essences* on page 154.)

JAPANESE MARTINI
CREATED BY SUNTORY, LIMITED

Shake

3 oz. (90 ml)
Suntory Juhyo Shochu
(vodka)

I splash
Suntory Green Tea Liqueur

fresh mint leaf

ESSENTIAL JAPANESE PHRASES:

Sumi ma sen. Matini, o kudasai.
(Translation: Excuse me. A Martini, please.)

Oribu o irette kudasai.
(Translation: Please put in an olive.)

Lemon no kawa o irette kudasai.
(Translation: Please put in a lemon skin.)

There's more to Tokyo nightlife than eating your fill of sushi, yakitori, or sukiyaki and catching a Kabuki theatre performance. Our friend Hideo took us out on the town, despite our severe case of jet lag. The twelve hour time difference was only a minute portion of what turned out to be an eye-opening experience. After dining in at a Roppongi country-style restaurant on fresh sea bass, grilled prawns, and Asahi beer, we proceeded to the first cocktail bar, where we found out our guide's nickname was Scotch Up. Somehow we found ourselves in a karaoke bar after a few rounds, with Scotch Up asking which bottles to buy for us. Within minutes we were dubbed Martini and Extra Dry, and a pair of bottles were added to the shelf in front of us with our names on them. It's much cheaper in Japanese bars to buy a whole bottle, and have them hold onto it for you, unless the people you're drinking with think it's high time everybody finished their bottles. *Kan-pai*!

We were all set for a good night's sleep by four in the afternoon and finally in bed by midnight. At 4 A.M. we were both wide awake and inexplicably starving. Luckily, the Tokyo Fish Market is open at that hour, as the fishing boats roll in round the clock, and the finest and freshest of the catch is served up right there–as raw as it was in the water.

THE ALASKA

With its unmistakably golden hue, it's easy to speculate that the 1930s cocktail–The Alaska (aka: The Bijou)–was named after the gold that led so many prospectors up to that frozen frontier at the turn of the century. The legends of nuggets as large as paving stones have faded, and mining has become a corporate enterprise; now Alaska has become legendary for its spirited individualists and its Martinis.

North of 60° there's an august body of aficionados known as the Fraternal Order of the Saturday Afternoon Martini Brethren. Founded in Dawson City, Yukon, the original members were transient summer workers who inhabited the town in 1995, gathering to promote, savor, and talk about Martinis.

The Order believes that the Martini is at risk of losing its style and grace among the younger generation (the members themselves range in age from 18 to 28); so they meet to enjoy and gab about their favorite drink. Part of the initiation is to contribute at least one anecdote involving the elixir, use its name in context as often as possible, and of course to drink gin Martinis. (Public consumption of vodka Martinis would be grounds for dismissal.)

This "old boys club" (which has one female founding member) chose Tagish Elvis as their spiritual leader. Elvis travels the Yukon in his baby blue Cadillac with a karaoke machine, entertaining unsuspecting crowds. Elvis also believes that aliens came down to earth and told him

Shake

2 oz. (60 ml)
Bombay Sapphire Gin

I splash
Yellow Chartreuse

I dash
Angostura Bitters

lemon twist

Along this same theme, we devised **The 180** (the approximate number of spices and flavorings used to make the ingredients) blending 2 oz. (60 ml) Bombay Sapphire Gin, I oz. (30 ml) Yellow Chartreuse, and I dash Angostura Bitters.

Our favorite arctic potable –a **True North**–combines 2 oz. (60 ml) Finlandia Vodka, I splash peppermint schnapps, and a sugar cube garnish.

WAITER THERE'S A TENTACLE IN MY MARTINI!

Some of the more unusual Martini garnishes out there: a smoked baby octopus tentacle, a cornichon, a squash blossom, a preserved human toe (not to be eaten), a clove of garlic, a Gummi Bear, a pickled tomatillo, a Hershey's Kiss, a kumquat, caviar, a hazelnut, a radish, a pickled quail egg, and an anchovy.

he was the real Elvis. He switched from Martinis to gin-and-tonics when his fifth wife left him, but he still hangs out with the Brethren.

The demand for Martinis up in the Yukon is so great that the Westmark Hotel in Dawson City hired master Martini mixologist Chris Dore from "down south" and a cigarette girl named Frenchie to run their dress-code-enforced Mercury Lounge nights.

The Westmark Hotel is also home to the exclusive Sour Toe Cocktail Society. To become a member, you have to drink your favorite cocktail garnished with a preserved human toe, letting the toe touch your lips at least once. At last count the membership was over 12,450.

A CAJUN COMBUSTION ENGINE

CREATED BY JIM HALL

Singer Jimmy Buffett croons about a Cajun Martini in his song, "We Are the People Our Parents Warned Us About." But where did this little slice of liquid fire come from? Renowned Louisiana chef Paul Prudhomme is often cited as the inventor of the Cajun Martini–although by his own admission, it was unintentional. As he stated in a recent interview:

> We actually started it as a joke because we didn't want to serve hard liquor and we had a license and we wanted to maintain the license as part of the agreement with the landlord...so...we put a cayenne pepper and a jalapeño pepper into a bottle of vodka and a bottle of gin and put a little vermouth in the serving. And I think the first one[s] lasted about three months. Then all of a sudden...we were selling two or three gallons a night.

Fortunately the genius of this creation wasn't lost on its creator, and Prudhomme quickly came out with his own line of ready-to-pour bottles of Cajun Martinis.

What is all this Cajun stuff? Sometimes we forget that the rest of the world doesn't have Louisiana in its living room and Mexico right next door. So for those of you who don't immediately see what's so funny about Chevy marketing their Nova model south of the border (which in Spanish, roughly translates to "it doesn't go"), a jalapeño is a little green chili that might be considered more appropriate

Shake

3 oz. (90 ml) pepper-infused Bombay Sapphire Gin

pickled serrano chili

(See *Instilled Essences* on page 154.)

"I only drink Martinis to cure what ails me."
"Why, what ails you?"
"Absolutely nothing. That's how well they work!"

Although everyone has memories they'd love to relive, sometimes it's the moments we'd never want to repeat that are the most memorable. We were sitting in Naves Bar on a sunny afternoon in Fairfax, California, when "shaken" took on a whole new meaning. Steve the bartender had just loaded up a shaker and put the lid on it when a tremor hit. We'll never know if he was paralyzed with fright, or the coolest bartender in the world at that moment, but with the room rolling and the bottles rattling, he just stood there motionless for half a minute holding the lid on the shaker. When it was over, he didn't say a word—or give the drink a single extra shake. He simply strained the contents into a waiting glass, slid it across the bar to the person who'd ordered it (and finally emerged from under a table to claim it), and wiped down the bar. Needless to say, we ordered our next round stirred.

for use in massage balm. But we love nibbling them to remind ourselves (through the ensuing agony) just how wonderful life really is. Cajun cooking –though it traces some of its roots back to France–is truly unique to the bayous of the Deep South.

If you're still wincing at the challenge of drinking chili-laced spirits, think about the fact that they're certainly an improvement over the 1930s version of a peppery Martini. The Miner's Cocktail consisted of two jiggers of gin, a splash of lemon juice, and two hefty pinches of fresh-ground black pepper.

Jeffrey Smith's **Cajun Martini**, which has also been dubbed **The Inferno**, blends 1 jigger Stolichnaya Pertskova, 1 splash olive juice, and a stuffed green olive garnish.

The **Peppertini** at Oliver's at The Mayflower Park Hotel blends 2 oz. (60 ml) Absolut Peppar Vodka over ice rinsed with 1 splash Cinzano Dry Vermouth. Red and black pepper flakes are sprinkled on top and a marinated olive is added as garnish.

Sean Hamilton's **Spicy Hamilton** gets its kick from Tabasco sauce, mixing 2 oz. (60 ml) Skyy vodka, 1 oz. (30 ml) Cinzano Dry Vermouth, and 3 drops Tabasco sauce. Rim the glass with lime and top the mix with a lemon twist.

The **Mansion Martini** served at the Mansion at Turtle Creek in Dallas uses a tequila rinse for the ice, shakes up 3 oz. (90 ml) Bombay Sapphire Gin, and garnishes it with jalapeño pepper-filled olive.

Lola's **Pepper Spray** shakes up 3 oz. (90 ml) vodka infused with tri-colored peppercorns. (See *Instilled Essences* on page 154.)

The Wake-Up Call was our first major attempt at infusing vodka with fresh spices. We'd sampled some interesting combinations at our local lounge (where gallon-sized glass jars of fruit-infused vodkas proudly stood behind the bar), but it wasn't until a blizzard shut down the entire city for a few days that we tried making our own infusion. (After all, the bars and grocery stores were shut tighter than a drum, leaving us to our own devices and the contents of our refrigerator.)

The result was exactly what the doctor ordered: the blood-warming spiciness was a welcome tonic during the frozen days that followed. In fact, it was so effective, we built three snowmen in subfreezing temperatures without getting frostbitten.

Shake

2 oz. (60 ml)
vodka infused with fresh
ginger slices and lemon
twists

1 splash
Korean ginseng extract

lemon twist

(See *Instilled Essences* on page 154.)

The **Wild Ginger** made at the Wild Ginger Restaurant in Seattle pours 3 oz. (90 ml) vodka infused with fresh ginger with a lemon twist garnish as their signature Martini.

The **Olympic Gold** at The Garden Court in the Four Seasons Olympic blends 1 oz. (30 ml) each of both Bombay Sapphire Gin and Absolut Citron Vodka, splashes of Canton Ginger Liqueur and Martel Cordon Bleu Champagne. (See *Distilled Essences* on page 118.)

DISTILLED ESSENCES
FLAVORED-VODKA MARTINIS

AVAILABLE DISTILLED FLAVORED VODKAS

CINNAMON:
Stoli® Zinamon

COFFEE:
Stoli® Kafya

CRANBERRY:
Finlandia Cranberry

CURRANT:
Absolut Kurant

LEMON:
Absolut Citron, Stolichnaya Limonnaya, Smirnoff Citrus Twist

ORANGE:
Stolichnaya Ohranj

PEACH:
Stoli® Persik

PEPPER:
Absolut Peppar, Stolichnaya Pertskova

PINEAPPLE:
Finlandia Pineapple

RASPBERRY:
Stoli® Razberi

STRAWBERRY:
Stoli® Strasberi

VANILLA:
Stoli® Vanil

Russia was a cold, austere place when Peter I became its monarch in 1682. From the day he first took the throne, Peter was known to be a workaholic with a limitless capacity for drinking and open contempt for political or religious pomp and circumstance. He'd built quite a reputation before he turned twenty-five years old. That's when he took a sixteen-month Grand Tour of Western Europe.

Travelling incognito, Peter made his way through Germany, Austria, the Netherlands, and England. Instead of bringing back conventional souvenirs like sculptures or paintings, the young Czar returned with a treasure-trove of western technological advances, customs, fashions, cuisine, and a full entourage of craftsmen and advisors. Peter (who by this time had earned his nickname, Peter the Great) had his culture army build a remarkably beautiful city–St. Petersburg–based on his own opulent architectural designs.

Besides instilling a new sense of style and grace into the Russian cultural landscape, Peter distilled his personal version of the national drink–vodka–with his newly acquired taste for Western flavors like pepper, berries, and spices. Three centuries later, Peter the Great's tastes have inspired a whole collection of modern Martinis.

Unlike infused flavors, which impart oils, pulp, sediment, and juices into the previously pure spirit, distilled essences acquire their characteristics in the actual manufacturing process. They preserve the spirit's integrity and strength by taking the best of the fermented grain and the fruit or spice, and wedding their tastes together in a colorless form. Style is still an essential element, especially in Martini culture. When it comes to mixology, flavored vodkas offer the ultimate way to create a Martini repertoire that exudes individuality.

AUTHENTIC RUSSIAN VODKA FLAVORED WITH ALL-NATURAL EXTRACTS OF MADAGASCAN AND INDONESIAN VANILLA BEANS.

THE DREAMSICLE

CREATED BY SET 'EM UP JOE

Shake

3 oz. (90 ml)
Stolichnaya Ohranj Vodka

1 splash of each:
Liqueur 43 and orange
juice

1 dash
heavy cream

orange slice

The signature Martini at **Becco's** blends 1.5 oz. (45 ml) Stoli® Ohranj Vodka, 0.75 oz. (22.5 ml) Martini & Rossi Sweet Vermouth, and splashes of Curaçao and Campari.

The **Muscovy Martini** blends 1 oz. (30 ml) each of both Stoli® Zinamon and Stolichnaya Ohranj vodkas, 0.5 oz. (15 ml) each of both Triple Sec and orange juice, garnished with a pinch of ground cinnamon.

Okay, so here's the one drink in the book that we do not consider to be part of the Martini species. Why's it here? Because it was so good! Cream, Shakespeare often said, doth not a Martini make. (Maybe that wasn't Shakespeare, but he's in no position to deny it.)

Creamsicles are one of those favorite flavors from childhood. Rich vanilla ice cream surrounded by a layer of orange sherbet was the perfect addition to any summer afternoon. The dreamsicle is the ultimate grown-up version.

It has a lot less sugar than a Creamsicle, although it's still got a lot of cream. We tried it with skim but, unlike cappucinos–which are better with skim milk–Dreamsicles need cream for that deliciously rich flavor. It even lends itself to something we'd never recommend for a real Martini: if you toss the ingredients into a blender with a cup of ice you can pile it up in a Martini glass to make the ultimate adult snowcone. If you can't find Liqueur 43, Cointreau works pretty nicely. And if this whole cream concept isn't quite what you had in mind, substitute a generous splash of Stoli® Vanil. It gives the drink a surprisingly similar taste, and also brings down the calories.

As a child growing up in Chicago's Rush Street district during its early 1960s cocktail heydays, I witnessed a lot of party scenes that could've been outtakes from *The Graduate* or *Barefoot in the Park*. Hugh Hefner had just opened the original Playboy Club on Walton Street, and the local nightclubs–Mr. Kelly's and the Gate of the Horn–were filled to capacity daily until 4 A.M. Who had to guess what adults did for fun at night? All I had to do was watch the nightly parade of revelers from my bedroom window.

One evening I'd gone upstairs to the indoor swimming pool, only to find myself surrounded by people in tuxedos and the latest Chanel evening dresses who–Martinis in hand and fully dressed –proceeded to leap into the pool. Even the hostess–a famous advice columnist (if you've read an American newspaper in the past decade, you probably know who I mean)–took the plunge in her peach-colored silk evening pajamas.

This Martini captures a bit of that night, as long as you don't water it down in the pool.

Shake

2 oz. (60 ml)
Bombay Sapphire Gin

1 oz. (30 ml)
Stoli® Persik Vodka

orange slice

Our **Kiev Spring**:
2 oz. (60 ml) Stoli® Strasberi Vodka, 1 oz. (30 ml) Stoli® Persik Vodka, and 1 dash fresh lemon juice.

Our **Georgian Twist** mixes 2 oz. (60 ml) Stoli® Strasberi Vodka and 1 splash Stolichnaya Limonnaya Vodka. While our **Blanche DuBois** replaces Limonnaya with Stoli® Vanil Vodka.

Clarke Trevett's **The Squeeze** pours 6 oz. (180 ml) of freezer-chilled Absolut Citron Vodka topped with lemon-cured olives.

ALEXANDER NEVSKY MARTINI

CREATED BY CARILLON IMPORTERS, LIMITED

Shake

2 oz. (60 ml)
Stoli® Razberi Vodka

1 oz. (30 ml)
Bombay Sapphire Gin

4 fresh raspberries and a
few drops of framboise or
kirschwasser

Our **Vladivostok** combines 2 oz. (60 ml) Stoli® Strasberi Vodka, 1 oz. (30 ml) Stoli® Razberi Vodka, 1 dash Macallan Scotch, and an orange twist garnish.

Our **Petrograd** uses 2 oz. (60 ml) Stoli® Razberi or Strasberi Vodka, 1 splash fresh lime juice, and a fresh berry garnish.

Our **Nureyev** mixes 2 oz. (60 ml) Stoli® Razberi Vodka, 1 oz. (30 ml) Stolichnaya Ohranj Vodka, and 1 splash Stoli® Vanil Vodka.

Wish we could remember which bar we were in when we first tried this drink. But it was the third or fourth bar of the evening, and we'd lost all our Polaroids when we left them in the fifth or sixth taxi. (They're great evidence: the perfect answer to that nagging questions: "Where was I last night?") The waitresses were all wearing this year's little black dresses, barely covering last year's little tattoos. The patrons in this little basement hideaway were sporting everything from tuxes and velvet slip dresses to skintight polyester turtlenecks under vintage silk paisley smoking jackets à la Hugh Hefner and taffeta, shoulderless cocktail frocks accessorized with matching French stiletto high heels and requisite black cigarette holders.

We hadn't ordered a round of Alexander Nevskys (or anything else for that matter) when our waitress placed a pair of these raspberry cocktails on our table. While you may not be able to get a horse to drink, you can always lead us to a new cocktail and we'll cooperate! The delicate taste was definitely worth repeating three more times. We never did figure out where we'd been (or what happened to the Polaroids) but we finally got the recipe.

MIKHAIL'S MARTINI
CREATED BY CARILLON IMPORTERS, LIMITED

When we heard about Mikhail's Martini, neither of us could wait to try combining vanilla- and coffee-flavored vodkas. Maybe it was the result of being surrounded by espresso bars everywhere we go, but the mix was even better than we'd imagined. It's rich but not sweet, and in varying proportions tastes a lot like Irish cream liqueur (without the extra calories) and coffee liqueur (without the sugar).

Nothing like a good Martini to allow you to indulge yourself, without dieting. The latest three-button suits and hourglass shifts aren't kind to out-of-place bulges. Besides, clear drinks are another obvious fashion-conscious plus: you don't have to concern yourself with color coordinating your most visible accessory.

Stir

2 oz. (60 ml)
Stoli® Kafya Vodka

1 splash
Stoli® Vanil Vodka

a few coffee beans

A man must defend his wife, his home, his children and his Martini.
—Jackie Gleason

Our own variation—the **Anastasia**—uses 2 oz. (60 ml) Stoli® Kafya Vodka and 1 oz. (30 ml) Stoli® Vanil Vodka.

The spicier **Patricia Petrosk** mixes 2 oz. (60 ml) Stoli® Kafya Vodka, 1 oz. (30 ml) Stoli® Vanil Vodka, and 1 dash Stoli® Zinamon Vodka.

The **Natasha Rambovna** is a mochaccino delight, combining 2 oz. (60 ml) Stoli® Kafya Vodka, 1 oz. (30 ml) Stoli® Vanil Vodka, and 0.5 oz. (15 ml) Godiva Chocolate Liqueur.

Lola's makes **The Three Evils** with 3 oz. (90 ml) espresso-bean infused vodka and 1 splash Godiva Chocolate Liqueur. (See *Instilled Essences* on page 154)

Shake

2 oz. (60 ml)
Stoli® Strasberi Vodka

1 splash of each:
Cinzano Dry Vermouth and
Cinzano Sweet Vermouth

fresh strawberry

The **Classic Bloodhound** from the 1930s mixes the same amounts of both types of vermouth, gin, and a fresh, whole strawberry garnish. Later versions also included 1 splash strawberry liqueur.

Our **Siberian Express** mixes 2 oz. (60 ml) Stoli® Razberi Vodka, 1 oz. (30 ml) Stoli® Vanil Vodka, and 1 splash Godiva Chocolate Liqueur.

Our **North Beach** replaces the raspberry vodka with the same amount of Stoli® Strasberi Vodka.

We'd love to claim we invented the Bloodhound. However, this drink dates back to the 1930s. Strawberry-flavored vodka adds a whole new dimension to the recipe. Since it's not sweet like a strawberry liqueur, it adds a lot more taste and aroma than a strawberry garnish could ever do on its own without losing the peppery essence that vodka brings to a Martini.

A frozen strawberry makes a great garnish. For best results, trim the tops off, and freeze them yourself. (While they're ideal for making margueritas and daiquiris, the ones in the grocer's frozen food section often get knocked around in transit and aren't as presentable.)

One great mistake that we made was using frozen strawberries in the shaker as a substitute for ice cubes. It made a cloudy mess out of our drinks, although the strawberries tasted great afterwards.

The perfect snack to go with a Bloodhound is a plate of strawberries that've been marinated in strawberry-flavored vodka for a few hours. Leave them out to marinate, then chill them just before serving. (Mint leaves make a good garnish.)

PASSIONATE ELIXIRS
MARTINIS BUILT FOR TWO

Hovering near the top of the Top Ten Things That Two Can Do Better Than One is having a Martini. If you haven't gotten the hint yet, Martinis have sex appeal. What other drink inspires discussions about smooth fire, Fred Astaire dance steps, cool jazz, and candlelit surroundings? Martinis spell sophisticated, seductive romance, especially when you make them for two.

A romantic tête-à-tête isn't difficult to arrange. All you need is a dose of Hollywood inspiration: set the stage, check your props (the bar is set up and stocked, glasses are sparkling clean, the food is ready, the flowers are in position), make sure your costume fits, call make-up if you must, brush up on your mixology, and rehearse your sexiest lines. Don't forget to remove your roommates, drop the kids off at grandma's house, turn the phone or the fax off, and switch the background music on. And make sure that the one you love is in the mood.

We've found a few memorable scenarios and double-sized recipes made with the finest ingredients to ignite your imagination. But we're sure you have a couple of your own, too.

A shy English major was surprised when the school's best-looking cheerleader accepted his invitation to go out for Martinis.

By the third drink he'd completely run out of small talk. In desperation he asked, "Do you like Kipling?"

To his surprise, her eyes lit up, and she smiled for the first time all night, but she didn't answer.

He leaned closer and asked again, "Do you?"

"Well, I don't know," she replied between giggles, "I've never kippled."

ROYAL WEDDING

CREATED BY OLIVER'S AT THE MAYFLOWER PARK HOTEL

Makes two servings

Shake

6 oz. (90 ml)
Stolichnaya Vodka

1 splash
Chivas Regal Scotch

vermouth-marinated olives
or lemon twist

Pour the scotch into a
glass shaker. Swirl to coat
and drain. Fill the shaker
with ice. Pour vodka over
the ice and shake. Place
garnish in a chilled glass
and pour.

This cocktail can also
be built with Bombay
Sapphire Gin.

Our own **Windsor
Wedding** replaces the
blended Scotch with
Macallan Scotch.

There's nothing like a regal matrimonial ceremony. The meeting of two stately spirits–vodka and Scotch–is definitely worth sharing with the one you love. After a full day of skiing, there's nothing more romantic than snuggling up in front of a roaring fireplace and sipping a couple of après-ski Martinis like the Royal Wedding. To revive both of your spirits and energies, think about how romantic it would be to nibble from a tray of delectable wintertime delights like smoked salmon, sharp cheeses, fresh pears, and a few chocolate truffles while a samba plays in the background. Think about the Alpine love scenes in *The Spy Who Loved Me* and *On Her Majesty's Secret Service*.

So you're not athletically inclined. You could consider taking a scene right out of a 1960s *Playboy* or *Cosmopolitan* article. Spend an evening in an oak-panelled lounge listening to a jazz trio playing "Stormy Monday" while you nestle in a love seat or a pair of oversized armchairs and share a couple of Martinis.

LA DOLCE VITA
CREATED BY HOLGER FAULHAMMER

Maybe you're feeling lyrical. A candlelit Italian dinner for two has melted many romantic hearts, so there must be something to it. You can start off by sharing a round of rosy-hued La Dolce Vitas while you nibble at a fresh antipasto. For the main course, forget the pizza, go for pasta and a salad (unless your culinary imagination and budget sends you in the direction of a saltim bocca alla romana or a portabello mushroom risotto). To set the mood, play some light opera or something sung by Tony Bennett, Frank Sinatra, Nat King Cole, or Dean Martin. If it worked for the world's great Italian lovers–Marcello Mastroianni, Rudolph Valentino, Giancarlo Giannini–who knows what the evening will have in store?

A rustic Tuscan picnic is another ideal Italian-style setting that's shown great promise. A picnic basket filled with fruit, fresh bread, cheeses, sausages, and a portable bar is all you need to make a day in the country a special occasion.

Makes two servings

Shake

3 oz. (90 ml) of each: Bombay Sapphire Gin, Martini & Rossi Extra-Dry Vermouth, and Italian dry white wine

1 dash Campari

The Garden Court's **Copper Illusion** uses 4 oz. (120 ml) Beefeater Gin, 0.5 oz. (15 ml) each of both Cointreau and Campari.

Oliver's **Sterling Gold** mixes 4 oz. (120 ml) Tanqueray Sterling Vodka and 0.5 oz. (15 ml) Tuaca Liqueur.

The **Negroni** mixes 3 oz. dry gin and 0.5 oz. (15 ml) each of both Campari and Cinzano Sweet Vermouth.

Makes two servings

Shake

4 oz. (120 ml)
Stolichnaya Gold Vodka

0.5 oz. (15 ml) of each:
Martini & Rossi Dry
Vermouth and Wild Turkey
Bourbon

lemon twist or a
maraschino cherry

Southerners have a grand reputation for being real ladies and gentlemen. (After all, Scarlet O'Hara and Rhett Butler were such innocent, civilized angels.) But you don't have to follow suit by serving up mint juleps on the plantation verandah or hanging up clusters of Spanish moss in the trees around your house to create a romantic Southern setting.

You could also head up north to Nashville where the smooth, genteel life can be experienced over a delicious fried chicken picnic by the riverbank. You can be casually romantic in this leisurely atmosphere. Wear your jeans and ginghams. (Leave that white linen suit and white chiffon tea dress for visits to the folks down home.) Accompanied by a few smooth Nashville Martinis and a slow dance to the "Tennessee Waltz," a lazy-afternoon picnic under the willows can transform even the most stressed-out Northern attitudes into gentler, more amorous states of mind.

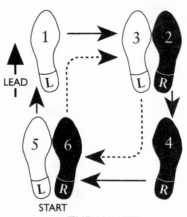

THE WALTZ

The nations south of the border produced some of the world's sexiest dances like the mambo, samba, rumba, cha cha, and lambada. So brush up on your ballroom footwork and smoldering glances if you plan to follow in the footsteps of the Latin ladies like Carmen Miranda or Sonia Braga and their male counterparts: Ricardo Montalban, Fernando Lamas, and Antonio Banderas. A double Martini served in an extra large glass is the perfect way to share a sensual Mezcatini together.

And from Spain, tapas (which means "small tastes") treats like grilled chicken breast in garlic or fried baby squid are mouthwatering temptations that won't douse your fiery passions. Background music can run the whole gamut from Carmen Miranda's rendition of "Tico Tico" to Stan Getz's "Girl from Ipanema" or the theme from *Black Orpheus*. A sultry sax performance by Gato Barbieri or a saucy salsa by Ruben Blades are some interesting options. Whatever you do, don't try to impress your loved one with your bongo interpretation of "Babaloo."

Makes two servings

Shake

4 oz. (120 ml)
Stolichnaya Vodka

1 oz. (30 ml)
Mescal

2 dashes
Rose's Lime Cordial

orange twist

Rinse the shaker with the Tuaca Liqueur. Add ice and vodka. Shake until ice cold. Strain and garnish.

The Mighty Niagara's **Tequini** combines equal parts of tequila, vodka, dry vermouth, 1 dash Angostura Bitters, and a lemon twist garnish.

FRENCH KISS

Makes two servings

Shake

3 oz. (90 ml)
Stolichnaya Gold Vodka

1 oz. (30 ml)
Kina Lillet Blanc

2 oz. (60 ml)
Moët et Chandon Brut
Imperial Champagne

orange twist

Rinse the shaker with Lillet. Add ice and vodka. Shake until cold. Strain and garnish. Add champagne just before serving.

Our own **Odessa Splash** uses 4 oz. (120 ml) Stoli® Persik Vodka, 2 oz. (60 ml) Veuve Clicquot Ponsardin Champagne, and a lemon twist garnish.

They say that the French live for love. They taste its delicacy like a lemon soufflé and its richness like a hand-rolled chocolate truffle. The French breathe a passionate air that very much resembles a bottle of champagne. They are aloof and self-contained until they encounter the source of their desire. Then they explode in a burst of bubbling ecstasy. A Martini has that same cool sensuality. But can you imagine the effect when a splash of champagne is added to that glass of liquid satin? Now that's a French Kiss.

Surround that pale, effervescent image with a table for two dressed in white linen with a single burning white candle and a single long-stemmed red rose. Serve a sensuous dessert like a dish of fresh strawberries kissed with a dollop of whipped cream or crème fraîche. (The two of you can reenact Nastassja Kinski's luscious strawberry scene from *Tess of the d'Urbervilles*, or just whisper sweet nothings in each other's ear.)

The tempestuous tango may have been invented in Buenos Aires, but its coolly detached sensuality reminds us of dimly lit Parisian bistros. (We're not discussing the *Last Tango in Paris* here.) We're talking about playing a sultry instrumental performed by Astor Piazolla or The French Hot Quintet and doing a close, barefoot tango. Study Charles Boyer's role as Pepe Le Moko in the 1940s movie, *Algiers*. (Unlike his cartoon skunk counterpart, Pepe Le Pew, the sexy Le Moko always got his woman.) His discrete yet steamy charm swept Hedy Lamarr off her feet when he invited her to come with him to the Kasbah.

What we've been talking about all along is a love affair. It may last for a moment or a lifetime, who knows? But like any great passion, it should be eloquent and elegant. The memory should last an eternity.

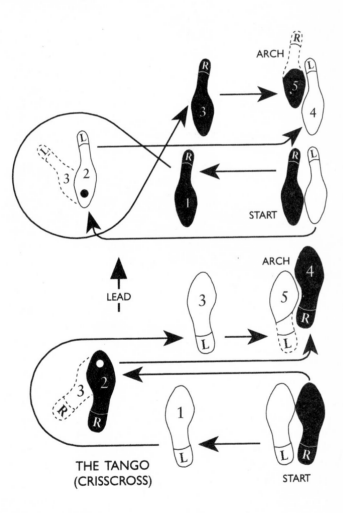

THE TANGO
(CRISSCROSS)

CHAPTER THREE

GUEST LIST

Modern Martini Culture

It's always happy hour somewhere in the world, the rest is just good timing.

The faces may change (even the fashions may change), but in cocktail culture the party's been going on for over a century, and it just seems to get better. If you're anywhere near a major city, chances are that there's a lounge, bar, restaurant or party for every night of the week, whether you're in the mood to wear a tux or a vintage bowling shirt. If you feel like standing out in the crowd, just go for the opposite of what the evening calls for–though it's generally more fun to be overdressed than underdressed.

"How is it," someone asked, "that such a simple cocktail like a Martini has so much mystique attached to it?" For the same reason that the Martini is the universal symbol for lounges and bars, it's more than a drink: it's a beacon, a statement, a warning of fun in progress. Along the way, it's picked up the best in music, fashion, and attitude.

MARTINI MUSIC
CLASSIC AND MODERN LOUNGE SOUNDS

They say that music soothes the savage beast. It also smoothes a gritty Martini and complements a perfect one. The Cocktail Age sounds of Bix Beiderbecke, Paul Whiteman & His Orchestra, Bing Crosby, Cole Porter, George Gershwin, Fats Waller, Cab Calloway, and Josephine Baker should be high on your list.

If you're new to the Lounge Music genre, check out a few CD anthologies from Capitol Records' Ultra-Lounge cocktail music series like *Mondo Exotica, Cha Cha De Amour, A Bachelor in Paris, Cocktail Caper, Saxophobia*, or *Mambo Fever*, before delving into specific artists.

Check out *Bachelor in Paradise*, a collection of MGM film hits, and Henry Mancini's greatest hits. For a touch of Polynesian tiki-heaven, classics sounds from the Martin Denny combo or Arthur Lyman's *Taboo* and *Hawaiian Sunset* from Rykodisc will transport you to the balmy beaches at Waikiki.

Juan Garcia Esquivel's *Space Age Bachelor Pad Music* and Pérez Prado & His Orchestra's *Mondo Mambo* are musts for Latin beat loungers. Xavier Cougat, Desi Arnaz, and Louie Prima (with Keelie Smith) should also be in your collection.

Occasionally we've been known to go for Carnival and samba sounds from Rio de Janiero: *the* album to own is *Getz/Gilberto* by Joào Gilberto and Stan Getz (which features haunting vocals by Astrid Giberto on songs like the

Here are a few notable musical birthdays to raise a Martini glass to:

Bix Beiderbecke, March 10
Billie Holiday, April 7
Ella Fitzgerald, April 25
Duke Ellington, April 29
Peggy Lee, May 26
Josephine Baker, June 3
Morgana King, June 4
Dean Martin, June 17
Lena Horne, June 30
Tony Bennett, August 3
Bobby Short, September 15
Connie Bennett, October 22
Lou Rawls, December 1
Sammy Davis, Jr., December 8
Frank Sinatra, December 12
Cab Calloway, December 24

"Girl from Ipanema"). We also look to Buenos Aires for tangos with Astor Piazolla's *Concierto Para Bandoneon*.

Francophiles will appreciate the sexy singing style of Serge Gainsbourg on hits like "Je t'aime" (accompanied by his wife Jane Birkin) or "Bonnie et Clyde"(a duet he recorded with Sixties sex-kitten Brigitte Bardot).

Anything recorded by Frank Sinatra, Tony Bennett, Mel Torme, Sammy Davis, Jr., Dean Martin, Dave Brubeck, Earl Fatha Heinz, Oscar Peterson, Cannonball Adderley, Lou Rawls, Harry Connick, Jr., and Nat King Cole is a must. And don't forget those lovely ladies like Ella Fitzgerald, Yma Sumac, Peggy Lee, Lena Horne, Carmen Miranda, and Edith Piaf.

New lounge sounds are being shaken up by bands like the Ulterior Motive Quartet, Axel Boys Quartet, Combustible Edison, the Cocktails, Love Jones, Friends of Dean Martinez, Stereolab, JaymzBee, and Tim Tomashiro. Direct from Japan, there's the band Pizzicato Five and an Art Van Damme Quintet CD entitled *Martini Time*.

If you need more ideas–or if you're fortunate enough to be musically inclined–and you're contemplating a jam session, check out Jack Lemmon on the bongos in the film *Bell, Book, and Candle*.

Finally, you'll want something upbeat for the morning after that isn't going to aggravate a hangover into existence. Some of our favorites are Anita O'Day's *Nightingale in Berkeley Square*. Squeeze's *Sweets for a Stranger,* "The Java Jive," and David Byrne's collection of Brazilian hits, entitled *O Samba*.

JACKET REQUIRED
MARTINI FASHIONS

We all know that any elixir looks more elegant when it's sipped from a wide-mouthed, stemmed cocktail glass, but if you're wearing a Mott the Hoople or Nirvana T-shirt with jeans from the same era in public, you might sour your compatriots' drinks and moods in a hurry.

If you want to look the part, there's about as many fashion options as there are Martini variations. But like the drink, these apparel designs seem to have a common root. It seems like every designer who's set out to make party clothes in the last forty years spent a few weekends watching Fellini's *La Dolce Vita* (or else their designs looked like they should have). Even without any discernable plot, the film –which centers around Marcello Mastroianni hopping from party to party–is a cocktail classic.

Other great big-screen sources for cocktail fashion and style include *Ocean's 11* (Frank Sinatra, Dean Martin, Sammy Davis, Jr., and Angie Dickinson), *Swingers* (a 1996 release, so if you missed it in the theaters go rent it! It's "Money, baby, money!"), *Breakfast at Tiffany's*, and any of the "Thin Man" movies (check out William Powell's shawl-collared blazers).

R.S.V.P.
MARTINI PARTY PLANNING

Martinis have been the life of the party since the 1860s when ostentatious banquets were held for just about every occasion. (Victorian etiquette dictated that our great grandparents had to have a reason to throw a party.) Devil-may-care Jazz Babies and Bright Young Things during the Cocktail Age preferred death to missing a good cocktail party (or being seen at a boring one). The early 1960s was an era when posh little get-togethers were part of urban and suburban tribal tradition–a sign of good breeding.

Fortunately, you don't need an excuse–or peer pressure–to gather friends together at your home to tip a few glasses. Serving Martinis for more than four people is enough cause for a celebration. So how do you throw a hot party? A big budget's not required, but organization, inspiration, and perfect presentation are. So let's map out a few details.

The first order of business is to pick a date. Experience has taught us not to schedule at-home fêtes during the work week unless you plan to hire a caterer to setup, serve, and clean up the remnants of your soirée. Fridays and Saturdays are the best days. They give you and your guests a chance to recuperate from the festivities. (You could add a bunch of cheap sunglasses to your party favors list so people can leave your abode at dawn in style. Plus, putting the whole party in shades adds a really amusing air of instant cool.)

SHAKEN NOT STIRRED

Once you've pinpointed the party date, it's time to make your biggest decision: what type of Martini party should you throw? Here are a few thoughts to get you started:

'Twas the hour before cocktails and all through the house, not a creature was stirring…or shaking…or pouring…

A sophisticated cocktail party–like something out of a feature film like *All About Eve* or *La Dolce Vita*–is ideal if you and your friends love dressing up in formal wear, tipping toasts with your best stemware, and–optionally–puffing the finest cigars and cigarettes.

A classy little come-as-you-are cocktail affair straight out of the pages of a Cocktail-Age Dashiell Hammett mystery or P.G. Wodehouse comedy is just the thing if your guests are coming over straight from work, going to a gala, cocktail hopping, or tearing themselves away from the television. For a few hours, the gang can kick up their heels to some Cotton Club jazz or wax philosophic about Hemingway adventures and basketball over a few masterfully mixed shakerfuls in your (living room) salon.

If the forecast calls for warm and sunny, you might want to throw a pool or even a rooftop party. Take a look at back *Playboy* issues from the 1960s for inspiration. The line-up of sportscars parked in front of your house and the bevy of babes in bikinis and cocktail dresses sauntering around the backyard will keep your neighbors talking till winter, especially if one of your guests performs some of the poolside antics from that film tribute to Swinging London-style, *Scandal*, or every James Bond film Sean Connery made.

One of our favorite party accessories

There's two jokers in every deck and at least one in every crowd, so here's a harmless practical joke for cocktail parties:

Buy a small package of Knox (clear) gelatin. Mix according to the instructions, substituting your regular proportions of gin and vermouth for half the water called for. As soon as it's ready, pour it over an olive or twist in a Martini glass, and put it in the fridge to chill.

When you're mixing drinks for your guests wait until the second or third round, then pour a tiny bit of fresh Martini on top of it and hand that one to someone as if it's a regular drink. If you're not serving at home, chances are you can get your favorite bartender to conspire with you if you set it up a day or two in advance.

is a Twister board. For larger parties, put two of them side-by-side. If you're hosting a pool party, it's the ultimate way to make sure everyone's wearing sunblock. Just spill a whole bottle out onto the Twister board and watch how quickly everyone gets covered. Now send out those invitations!

PARTY SUPPLIES

Before you stock up on your Martini party supplies, write your drink menu. Once you know how many guests are coming, start nailing down your recipes and then your shopping list.

The math is simple: you get fourteen 2 oz. pours of gin or vodka per 750 ml bottle. Let's say twelve guests are coming who seem to have a three-Martini limit. Subtracting a couple of designated drivers, you need to buy three bottles of gin or vodka or two bottles of each. (You'll either be rewarded with a leftover portion or the knowledge no one's calling you a dry well behind your back.)

Tag on one bottle of dry vermouth (that's fifty 0.5 oz. servings or just under 7000 drops per 750 ml bottle); and a bottle of each item (orange juice, Cointreau, champagne, liqueur, Scotch, etc.) needed to mix your menu. Remember, you can get away with small bottles of many of these.

Top your list with necessary garnishes—olives, pickled onions, lemons, oranges, etc.—and any requisite bar tools you might be missing like an extra cocktail shaker or mixing glass and cup with strainer, jiggers or shot glasses (one to accompany each shaker), Martini glasses (at least two per guest, though we prefer to have a few extras), and a couple of ice buckets filled with ice.

PARTY FOOD

Even we have to admit that men and women can't live by Martinis alone, they must have munchies. But we would never masticate conventional potato chips and pretzels while sipping our favorite elixirs. And we would never serve such mundane morsels to our Martini-savvy guests. The idea is to serve foods that'll reach an anesthetized palate without overwhelming it. With that in mind, we've developed a master list of single-handed finger food that we find ourselves reaching for before the throngs arrive:

- A selection of olives in a variety of sizes, stuffings, and marinades as well as some silver-skin cocktail onions
- Mixed nuts and Terra Chips (not your ordinary chips, please)
- A platter of cheeses like roquefort, stilton, sharp cheddar, and port wine cheddar (Skip the brie and gouda, they don't do so well with Martinis)
- Peppery cheese sticks
- Roasted garlic (*see recipe on page 140*)
- Crudité (raw veggies cut into bite-sized pieces) served with a horse-radish cream sauce (*see recipe on page 140*)
- Pâté maison or duck terrine served with baguette slices and cornichons
- Skewers of shrimp or prawns dusted cajun-style with a simple combo of spices (*see recipe on this page*) (Impress the socks off your friends by

---

EASY CAJUN SHRIMP BOUQUET
Makes 5 appetizer servings

1 lb. fresh medium-sized shrimp (about 30)

$\frac{1}{2}$ tablespoon salt

1 teaspoon ground black pepper

$\frac{1}{2}$ teaspoon ground cayenne pepper

$\frac{1}{2}$ teaspoon garlic powder

1 whole, fresh pineapple

Combine all dry ingredients in a salt shaker and set aside. Peel and de-vein shrimp. Place shrimp on the tips of individual 8-10" bamboo skewers. Bring 3 cups of water to a boil. Place skewers into the water, shrimp-end down. Reduce heat to medium and boil for 3 minutes. Slice the pineapple diagonally from the bottom to midway up the opposite side so that it will sit at an angle on a plate (leave the top on).

Remove the shrimp from the water, dust with the seasoning mix, and then stick the other ends of the skewers into the pineapple.

putting one shrimp on each skewer, then stab the back ends into a pineapple sliced diagonally to make a simple bouquet)

- Platter of steamed or fried dumplings delivered from the nearest Chinese restaurant

- Medallions of rare roast beef served on toast rounds and topped with Bernaise sauce

- Miniature potato and scallion pancakes topped with sour cream

- Smoked salmon platter served with capers, minced red onion, and bread rounds

- Raw oysters served on the half shell with fresh lemon wedges

- Caviar served with chopped egg, minced white onion, lemon wedges, and toast points

- Scallops or water chestnuts wrapped in pancetta (or regular bacon), that are skewered and grilled

- Miniature tart shells filled with curried chicken and topped with toasted walnuts and champagne grapes

- Toasted semolina or Italian bread slices topped with chopped fresh plum tomatoes, chopped garlic, extra virgin olive oil, wilted spinach, salt and pepper (aka: Bruschetta Fiorentina)

- Miniature tart shells filled with whole pecans and a pecan-pie glaze flavored with chocolate liqueur

- Fresh whole strawberries served with a small bowl of sour cream flavored with a pinch of ground cinnamon and dark brown sugar for dipping

Obviously you're not expected to serve everything on this list. We don't.

The idea is to pick a couple of the basics and a couple of fancier dishes. Or if you're not into cooking but someone who's coming is, you can always see if you can talk them into making one of these for you.

So where do you find the best moments that the cocktail culture has to offer? As one New Yorker who had a habit of crashing every party she passed on the street (and often got invited back for the next one) said, "Great moments aren't found. They're made."

"How can you marry that woman. She knows absolutely nothing about food."

"That's not true, we had a wonderful dinner last night."

"Oh? What'd she make?"

"Reservations. How could I be any happier?"

CHAPTER FOUR

HAPPY HOUR

The World's Best Martini Lounges

No matter where you go, chances are you can find a good Martini or two these days if you know where to look. Thanks to the revival of lounge culture (and innumerable subcultures), new watering holes are cropping up every month. The establishments listed here are a mix of ones that we've personally spent many happy hours in, and others that were highly recommended by visitors to our Web site.

What is it that makes a place ideal for Martini drinking? A talented and reputable mixologist behind the bar and comfortable surroundings are the criteria we use. The rest–good music, beautiful or unique people, great location, a well-stocked humidor, and an outstanding list of hard-to-find spirits–is just icing on the cake. (We just happen to like the places with a lot of icing.)

ICON KEY

A recipe from this establishment is featured in the text.

THE UNITED STATES

ARIZONA

Lateral Hazard, 4341 North 75 Street, Scottsdale (tel. 602/424-7100). Serious American food and the bartenders refresh your Martini in a new ice-cold glass when it starts to thaw.

CALIFORNIA

Bar Marmot, The Chateau Marmot, 1871 Sunset Boulevard, Hollywood (tel. 213/656-1010). Hotel bar in a renovated 1920s Hollywood landmark.

Bix Restaurant & Lounge, 56 Gold Street (Financial District), San Francisco (tel. 415/433-6300). One of the few bars around that still serves only classic gin- and vodka-based Dry Martinis; but those Martinis are served so perfectly mixed and chilled you really won't miss the others for a night.

The Blue Light, 1979 Union Street, San Francisco (tel. 415/922-5510). Crowded, lively club.

The Compass Rose, St. Francis Hotel, 335 Powell Street, San Francisco (tel. 415/397-7000). Elegant hotel lounge.

Cypress Club, 500 Jackson Street (in the Financial District), San Francisco (tel. 415/296-8555). Modern, really cool looking, a sort of cartoon of a supper club feel. Wednesday is Martini night!

The Derby Club, 4500 Los Feliz Boulevard, Hollywood (tel. 213/663-8979). Very chic, 1940s swing bar. Take a look at the movie *Swingers* to get the idea.

42°, 235 16th Street, San Francisco (tel. 415/777-5558). Modern cuisine restaurant with French/Spanish Mediterranean flair.

The Four Seasons Hotel Gardens, 690 Newport Center Drive, Newport Beach (tel. 714/759-0808). Better than the average hotel lounge. Wednesday is Martini night.

Good Luck Bar, 1514 Hillhurst Avenue, Hollywood (tel. 213/666-3524). The chic Hollywood after-hours Polynesian bar.

Harry Denton's Starlight Room, Sir Francis Drake Hotel, 450 Powell Street, San Francisco (tel. 415/392-7755). Old-time, elegant rooftop, hotel nightclub, featuring a ballroom dance floor and a magnificent view.

Joe's Café, 536 State Street, Santa Barbara (tel. 805/966-4638). Opened in 1928, it retains its old charm (and staff); known for great drinks, prime ribs, and steaks, with a full bar and a terrific bartender.

Julie's Supper Club, 1123 Folsom Street (south of Market Street), San Francisco (tel. 415/861-0707). Funky 50s-60s decor. Voted San Francisco's best Martinis in

1996 by the *San Francisco Guardian*.

Lava Lounge, 1533 North La Brea Avenue, Los Angeles (tel. 213/876-6612). Black-walled, hardcore lounge-lizard bar.

Little City, 673 Union Street (in North Beach area), San Francisco (tel. 415/434-2900). Laid-back American/Italian restaurant.

Lulu, 816 Folsom Street (south of Market Street), San Francisco (tel. 415/495-5775). Arty/modern restaurant.

McCormick & Schmick, 111 North Los Robles Avenue, Pasadena (tel. 818/405-0064). Cheeseburger/quesadilla restaurant.

The Mermaid, 4248 Martingale Way (near the pier), Hermosa Beach (tel. 714/851-5187). Piano bar.

Musso & Frank's, 6667 Hollywood Boulevard, Hollywood (tel. 213/467-5123). One of Hollywood's oldest restaurants.

Persian Aub Zam Zam, 1633 Haight Street, San Francisco (tel. 415/861-2545). Bruno is the bar's famous bartender who won't serve you if he doesn't like you.

Piped Piper Bar, The Palace Hotel, 2 New Montgomery Street, San Francisco (tel. 415/512-1111). The hotel lounge features a Maxfield Parrish mural, chess tables, and huge armchairs.

The Redwood Room, The Clift Hotel, Geary & Taylor Streets, San Francisco (tel. 415/775-4700). Classy hotel lounge paneled in redwood inlay.

The Tosca Café, 242 Columbus Avenue, San Francisco (tel. 415/391-1244). Restaurant/bar with an impeccable ancient jukebox.

Vesuvio's, 255 Columbus Avenue (at Jack Kerouac Alley, across from City Lights Bookstore), San Francisco (tel. 415/362-3370). Dark, art-and-literature Beat Generation bar.

COLORADO
Herman's Hideaway, 1578 S Broadway, Denver, (tel. 303/778-9916) Modern lounge decor with a neighborhood feel and great dancing: alternative, jazz, funk (the local paper, the *Westward*, has all the current music listings).

The Purple Martini, 1328 15th Street, Denver (tel. 303/820-0575). Great modern Martini lounge with about 80 Martinis on the menu.

FLORIDA
Delano Hotel, 1685 Collins Avenue, Miami Beach (tel. 305/538-7881) The Rose Bar in the Delano—a small living room that spills out into the lobby—is the place to see and be seen.

Les Deux Fontaines, 1230 Ocean Drive, Miami (tel. 305/672-7878) In the Ocean Front Hotel, it's laid back, intimate, couches, 25 Martinis on menu, plus cigars and a cigarette girl.

Mercury Restaurant, 764 Washington Avenue, Miami (South Beach) (tel. 305/532-0070) Modern industrial decor, Upscale American cuisine, and 40-50 Martinis on their menu.

GEORGIA
The Martini Club, 1140 Crescent Avenue NE, Atlanta (tel. 404/873-0794). Two-story Martini lounge in a renovated house.

ILLINOIS
Club Lucky, 1824 West Wabansia Avenue, Chicago (tel. 312/227-2300). River North young professional hangout.

Coq d'Or Restaurant & Lounge, Drake Hotel, 140 East Walton Street, Chicago (tel. 312/787-2200). Dark-paneled, hotel lounge. Pianist Buddy Charles is a Chicago landmark on his own.

Gibson's Steakhouse, 1028 North Rush Street, Chicago (tel. 312/266-8999). Near North Side steakhouse.

The Green Mill Cocktail Lounge, 4802 North Broadway Avenue, Chicago (tel. 312/878-5552). A 1930s decor jazz lounge.

Harry's Velvet Room, 534 North Clark Street, Chicago (tel. 312/828-0770). An Italian restaurant with deep burgundy sofas and a long dark wood bar.

Martini Ranch, 311 West Chicago Avenue, Chicago (tel. 312/335-9500). Bar serves a young, sophisticated Near North Side crowd.

Mashed Potato Club, 316 West Erie, Chicago (tel. 312/255-8579). Unique experience—it's a potato restaurant.

The Saloon, 200 East Chestnut Street, Chicago (tel. 312/280-5454). Theme-based Chicago steakhouse.

Set 'Em Up Joe, 22 West Elm Street, Chicago (tel. 312/280-4735). A 1950s piano bar with upstairs cigar lounge.

The Zebra Lounge, 1220 North State Street, Chicago (tel. 312/642-5140). Tiny Near North Side piano bar that's been around since the 1920s when it was a speakeasy.

LOUISIANA
The Bombay Club, The Prince Conti Hotel, 830 Conti Street, New Orleans (tel. 504/586-0972). Hotel lounge.

Kagan's Corner, 2311 Canal Street, New Orleans (tel. 504/821-0411). Small Irish pub in the French Quarter.

MARYLAND
The Owl Bar, 1 East Chase Street, Baltimore (tel. 410/347-0888). Inside the Belvedere, which was built in 1903, The Owl Bar boasts a 10.5 oz Martini! There's also a

Restaurant upstairs with a spectacular view.

Prime Rib, 1101 N. Calvert Street, Baltimore (tel. 410/539-1804). Prime rib/steak restaurant. Inside it's dark, candlelit, carpeted in leopard print, there's a piano player, and jackets are required.

MASSACHUSETTS
Grill 23 & Bar, 161 Berkeley Street, Boston (tel. 617/542-2255). Dark wood, brass, and leather upscale restaurant.

MICHIGAN
Flannagan's Irish Pub, 139 Pearl Street NW, Grand Rapids (tel. 616/454-7852). Irish pub.

220 Restaurant, 220 Merrill Street, Birmingham (tel. 810/645-2150). In the historic Edison Building, complete with its own collection of really cool antique electric lights.

MINNESOTA
The Loring Café, 1624 Harmon Place, Minneapolis (tel. 612/332-1617). The restaurant and bar overlooking Loring Park are filled with antiques and couches, giving the place an oversized living room feel. A small stage hosts live music every night ranging from classical to Greek to jazz to rock.

NEVADA
El Cortez, 235 West Second, Reno (tel. 702/324-4255). A seriously seedy old gambler bar.

Hardrock Hotel Casino & Bar, Hardrock Hotel, 4455 Paradise Road, Las Vegas (tel. 702/693-5000). Rock'n'roll casino bar.

Hilltop House, 3500 North Rancho Drive, Las Vegas (tel. 702/645-9904). Steak and lobster restaurant with a 35-year tradition.

The Rapscallion, 1555 South Wells, Reno (tel. 702/323-1211). One of Reno's only non-casino eating establishments.

NEW YORK
Bemelman's Bar, The Carlyle Hotel, 35 East 76 Street, New York (tel. 212/744-1600). Intimate hotel lounge.

The Blue Bar, The Algonquin Hotel, 59 West 44 Street, New York (tel. 212/840-6800). Classic hotel lounge that's still patronized by the Manhattan literary world.

Bubble Lounge, 228 West Broadway, New York (tel. 212/431-3433). Very chic Soho cocktail lounge.

Chaz & Wilson, 201 West 79 Street, New York (tel. 212/769-0100). Upper West side bar. Stingers, a great Motown-Stax-Memphis type review with four or five singers and a backup band plays on Wednesdays.

57/57, The Four Seasons Hotel, 57 East 57 Street, New York (tel. 212/758-5757). Elegant hotel lounge. Make reservations if you plan on spending a Friday or Saturday evening there.

The Four Seasons Restaurant, 99 East 52 Street, New York (tel. 212/754-9494). The ceiling above this modern 1950s bar is an eye-catcher: a sort of Damocles decor.

Global 33, 93 Second Avenue (between 5 and 6 Streets), New York (tel. 212/477-8427). Fun, East Village bar.

Jet Lounge, 286 Spring Street, New York (tel. 212/675-2277). Soho cocktail lounge.

Lucatelli's, 205 Elmira Road, Ithaca (tel. 607/273-0777). Italian restaurant.

Martini's, 810 Seventh Avenue (at 53 Street), New York (tel. 212/767-1717). Martinis are served in stemless glasses that rest in glass bowls filled with crushed ice at this modern restaurant.

Merchant's, 521 Columbus Avenue, New York (tel. 212/721-3689). Small but great Upper West Side bar.

Monkey Bar, 60 East 54 Street, New York (tel. 212/838-2600). Old, 1940s-style hotel lounge with a serious dress code.

Naked Lunch, 17 Thompson Street, New York (tel. 212/343-0828). Bar-lounge open 5 P.M.-4 A.M. Busy after 11:30 P.M. Ask for George, one of New York's

finest mixologists, to make your Martini.

95 School Street, 95 School Street, Bridgehampton (tel. 516/537-5555). Cozy Hamptons resort bar.

The Oak Bar, Plaza Hotel, 59 Street at Fifth Avenue, New York (tel. 212/759-3000). Classic hotel lounge that's still patronized by the Manhattan literary world.

Palm Too Restaurant, 840 Second Avenue, New York (tel. 212/687-7698). Well-known New York steak and lobster restaurant.

Peacock Alley, Waldorf-Astoria Hotel, 301 Park Avenue, New York (tel. 212/355-3000). Classic hotel lounge.

Pravda, 281 Lafayette Street, New York (tel. 212/226-4696). Elegant, modern basement outfitted with comfortable armchairs and chic Soho atmosphere. The wait can be up to 45 minutes on serious outing nights.

The Rainbow Room, 64th Floor, Rockefeller Center, 30 Rockefeller Plaza, New York (tel. 212/632-5000). One of New York's best Cocktail Age supper clubs overlooking Midtown. The view is great, the dress code is enforced, and the prices aren't as high as you'd expect. The bar opens at 5:30 or 6 P.M.

Tatou Restaurant, 151 East 50 Street, New York (tel. 212/753-1144). High class and very hip cabaret, jackets required. If Fellini had filmed *La Dolce Vita* in New York, Tatou might have been the backdrop for one of his nightclub scenes.

Trattoria Della Arte, 900 Seventh Avenue (between 56 and 57 Streets), New York (tel. 212/245-9800). Hip modern Italian restaurant and bar. Hard to miss, there's a huge plaster nose in the window.

21 Club, 21 West 52 Street, New York (tel. 212/582-7200). Classic New York restaurant.

Vermouth, 355 Amsterdam Avenue, New York (tel. 212/724-3600). Upper West Side Martini lounge.

Zip City Brewing, 3 West 18 Street, New York (tel. 212/366-6333). Microbrewery/bar/restaurant. Dark wood interior, huge brew kettles rise up from the center of the bar; food and Martinis are both first rate.

NEW JERSEY

Hofbrauhaus, Ocean Boulevard, Atlantic Highlands (tel. 908/291-0224). The view of New York City, Verrazano Bridge, and the Atlantic Ocean just past Sandy Hook from this restaurant is breathtaking.

OHIO

The Whiskey, 1575 Merwin Avenue, Cleveland (tel. 216/522-1575). Martini lounge.

Dilullo's Trattoria, 2130 Albertson Parkway, Cuyahoga Falls (tel. 330/928-4936). The restaurant has a '30s Art Deco decor.

Ken Stewart's Grille, 1970 West Market Street, Akron (tel. 330/867-2555). Steak and seafood restaurant that serves a great Octopus Martini.

OREGON

The Gypsy, 625 NW 21 Street, Portland (tel. 503/796-1859). This laid-back restaurant has upper and lower lounges. (The lower lounge is set aside for cigar aficionados.)

TEXAS

Bitter End Bistro & Brewery, 311 Colorado Street, Austin (tel. 512/478-2337). Restaurant/microbrewery that caters to a young professional crowd.

Boulevard Bistrot, 4319 Montrose, Houston (tel. 713/524-6922). This modern cuisine restaurant features local produce prepared with remarkable imagination.

Cedar Street, 208 West Fourth Street, Austin (tel. 512/708-8811). Cocktail lounge with cigar bar and live jazz.

The Mansion at Turtle Creek, 2821 Turtle Creek Boulevard, Dallas (tel. 214/559-2100). Elegant southwestern cuisine restaurant.

Martini Ranch, 2816 Fairmount, Dallas (tel. 214/220-2116) Avant/modern Martini lounge serving 40 types of vodkas.

WASHINGTON

The Georgian Room, Four Seasons Olympic Hotel, 411 University, Seattle (tel. 206/621-1700). Good on-site humidor and an elegant hotel lounge: tall, arched windows, plants, private sitting areas.

Oliver's, Mayflower Park Hotel, 405 Olive Way, Seattle (tel. 206/623-8700). This elegant, Edwardian room feels like a private club, but attracts hotel guests as well as a faithful crowd of regulars to sample the Martinis that are perennial winners of the Seattle Martini Competition.

Palace Kitchen, 2030 Fifth Avenue, Seattle (tel. 206/448-2001). Classy restaurant with a wrap-around bar.

Wild Ginger, 1400 Western Boulevard, Seattle (tel. 206/623-4450). Elegant, modern Asian restaurant.

WASHINGTON, D.C.

A.V. Ristorante Italiano, 607 New York Avenue NW (tel. 202/737-0550). The back of this Italian restaurant houses a beautiful marble bar.

Capital Lounge, 229-231 Pennsylvania Avenue SE (tel. 202/547-2098). A new Capitol Hill bar and grill that also has a cigar and Martini room.

WISCONSIN

Genna's Lounge, 105 W. Main St., Madison (tel. 608/255-4770). Biker/fern bar on the Capitol Square where the crowd plays Twister or listens to loud music.

CANADA

BRITISH COLUMBIA

The Blue Lizard Lounge, Waldorf Hotel, 1489 East Hastings Street, Vancouver (tel. 604/253-7141). A 1950s Polynesian lounge that transforms itself on every third Saturday with live "lounge moderne" music and limbo contests hosted by Maxine Von Minx.

Delilah's, 1739 Comox Street (in the Denman Place Mall), Vancouver (tel. 604/687-3424). Chic Edwardian restaurant in the West End.

The Drawing Room Dance Hall, 751 View Street (top floor), Victoria (tel. 604/920-7798). Young professional crowd nightclub.

Gerard's, The Sutton Place Hotel, 845 Burrard Street, Vancouver (tel. 604/682-5511). Elegant dark-oak paneled hotel lounge styled like a gentlemen's club.

Lola's at Century House, 432 Richards Street, Vancouver (tel. 604/684-LOLA [5652]). Rich, decadent setting of dark wood, candlelight, and phenomenal food.

The Mighty Niagara, Niagara Hotel, 435 West Pender Street, Vancouver (tel. 604/688-7574). On Wednesday nights, this very retro bar turns on the dress code, cranks up the lounge music, and serves up Polynesian style. Things start hoppin' after 10 P.M.

Monterey Grill, Pacific Palisades Hotel, 1277 Robson Street, Vancouver (tel. 604/688-0461). This elegant hotel restaurant has a comfortable lounge complete with fireplace.

The Purple Onion, 15 Water Street, Vancouver (tel. 604/602-9442). This dress-code enforced nightclub features dance music while the lounge serves up live jazz in a modern decor.

ONTARIO
Bar Babylon, 553 Church Street, Toronto (tel. 416/923-2626). Cozy little Martini lounge.

QUEBEC
Jello Bar (*La maison du martini*), 151 Ontario St. East, Montreal (tel. 514/285-2621). Hip bar with a 1950s/1960s decor.

THE YUKON
The Keno Lounge, The Westmark Hotel, Dawson City (tel. 403/993-5339). On Sunday and Monday nights, the Keno turns into the Mercury Lounge which features a dressier code and a cigarette girl named Frenchie. This is also the only place in the world where you can drink a dry martini with a human toe–the Sour Toe Cocktail–and for five dollars, join the notorious Sour Toe Cocktail Society. All you have to do is touch the toe to your lips. It's pretty easy to find–across from a fine dining restaurant called Marina's. (There are no street addresses in this town. Just ask a local who'll point the way.)

EUROPE

FRANCE
Harry's New York Bar, 5 Rue Danau, 2e, Paris (tel. 42/61-71-14). Lost Generation landmark in the Opéra district.

Le Dépanneur, 27 Rue Fontaine, 9e, Paris (tel. 40/16-40-20). Young professional crowd inhabits this Pigalle district bar.

GERMANY
Bar Am Lützowplatz, Am Lützowplatz, Berlin (tel. 030/2626-807). Chic American bar.

Casablanca, Parkhotel, Wiensenhüttenpl 28, Frankfurt (tel. 069/26970). Chic hotel lounge.

Havana, Hernnstrasse 3, Munich (tel. 089/291-884). Purposefully rundown Cuban dive that attracts a young, chic patronage.

Harry's New York Bar, Grande Hotel Esplanade, Am Lüttzzowusfer 15, Berlin (tel. 030/2547-8821). Hotel lounge with a piano bar.

Jimmy's Bar, Hessischer Hof Hotel, Ebert-Anlage 40, Frankfurt (tel. 069/614-559). Classy executive bar.

Schumann's Bar, Maximilianstrasse 36, Munich (tel. 089/229-268). Many locals consider this to be Germany's best "American bar."

GREAT BRITAIN
American Bar, The Savoy Hotel, The Strand, London WC2 (tel. 0171/836-4343). Classic Edwardian hotel lounge renowned for making the nation's top-notch classic Martinis.

Brown's Restaurant, Woodstock Road, Oxford (tel. 865/511995). Elegant restaurant that serves equally classic Martinis to a young, professional crowd.

Cocktail Bar, The Café Royal, 68 Regent Street, London W1 (tel. 0171/437-9090). Victorian bar that's maintained its decadence and decor since the days when playwright Oscar Wilde and artist Aubrey Beardesley drank there.

Henry Africa's Hothouse, 65 White Ladies Road, Bristol (tel. 117/923-8300). Chic cocktail lounge with a Safari decor.

Smollensky's on the Strand, 105 The Strand, London WC2 (tel. 0171/497-2101). Cocktail lounge that offers live jazz, food, and dancing.

ITALY
Amerini, Via della Vigna Nuova (near Via Tornabuoni), Florence. American bar that even makes a Pasini Express to order.

Calice, Via Clavature, Bologna. American bar with a good reputation.

Harry's Bar, Calle Vallaresso, San Marco 1323 Venice (tel. 041/528-57-77). Landmark café near the Plaza San Marco.

RUSSIA
Metropol Hotel, Teatralny Proezd 1/4, Moscow (tel. 095/927-6000 or 7501/927-1000 outside Moscow). Elegant hotel lounge situated across from the Bolshoi Theater.

National Hotel, 14/1 Okhotny Ryad, Moscow (tel. 095/258-7000). Hotel lounge with restored Russian Art Nouveau decor located across the street from Red Square.

Piano Bar Old Square, 8 Bolshoi Cherkassky Pereulok, Moscow (tel. 095/298-4688). Casual, 24-hour cocktail lounge that caters to a young crowd.

Savoy Hotel, Ul. Rozhdestvenka, Moscow (tel. 095/929-8500). Opulent hotel lounge that was built in 1912 and recently restored.

ASIA

JAPAN

Henry Africa, Akasaka Ishida Bldg., 2F, 3-13-14 Akasaka, Minato-ku, Tokyo (tel. 031/3585 -0149). Cocktail lounge with a Safari decor.

Highlander, Hotel Okura, 2-10-4 Toranomon, Minato-ku, Tokyo (tel. 03/3505-6077). Hotel lounge with an elegant 1960s decor.

The Old Imperial Bar, The Imperial Hotel, 1-1-1 Uchisaiwacho, Chiyoda-ku, Tokyo (tel. 03/3504-1111). Elegant hotel lounge.

INSTILLED ESSENCES
Infused-Vodka Martinis

GINGER INFUSED VODKA

1 pint grain vodka

1 oz. (28 g) fresh, thinly sliced ginger

3 large lemon twists

Transfer vodka into a canning jar. (Save the bottle.) Add ginger and twists. Seal the container and throw it in the fridge for overnight. Taste-test the mixture. (If it's too spicy, add more vodka.) Decant the liquid through a gold-mesh coffee filter back into its original bottle and place it in the freezer.

JALAPEÑO PEPPER INFUSED GIN

1 liter dry gin

3 jalapeño peppers, quartered

1 chipotle pepper (a smoked jalapeño pepper)

Transfer gin into a canning jar. Add peppers. Seal the container and throw it in the fridge for two weeks. Decant the gin through a gold-mesh coffee filter back into the bottle and place it the freezer. If it's too spicy add more gin.

If you love to experiment in the kitchen–or you're a chemistry major with a few spare moments–making your own infused vodkas rewards you with the fruits (and spices) of your labors. The first time we made an infusion, we realized that we'd created something different. But it was way too strong. No problem, we diluted it with more vodka. It turned out to be the perfect addition to an après-ski warm up Martini. (*See Wake-Up Call on page 117.*)

The recipe was simple. Transfer a pint of grain vodka to a clean, sterilized mason jar. Add sliced, fresh ginger and lemon twists. (*See ginger infusion instructions on this page.*) Close tightly and place the jar in the refrigerator overnight. Strain the liquid through a coffee filter (gold mesh ones are great for this) to get rid of the sediments and keep it in the freezer until you're ready to use it.

Originally, we made the mistake of infusing the mixture for three days and had to add nearly a cup of vodka to mellow it out. We learned quickly not to let chemistry take its course for too long. We visited a few bartenders who had mastered the art of infusion, taking notes on the proportion, balance, and time their potions were steeped. Some of these sages let their potions steep for weeks in warm climates. However, more health conscious ones advised us never to practice this form of alchemy.

Most infusions can be made in less than two weeks. Some can even be made overnight.

Back in our own kitchen, we pushed the envelope. We learned to make a lovely rose-colored cranberry infusion using sun-dried cranberries steeped overnight which makes the perfect Cosmopolitan. We also tried a remarkable sun-dried cherry infusion with orange twists. (*See cranberry and cherry infusion instructions on this page.*)

Fresh fruits require a different approach. Fill a quart-sized mason jar with fresh cranberries and cherries, d'anjou pear slices, plums, rose hips, limes, or key limes, then add your pint of vodka. This method can take up to four days to produce results. Unlike sun-dried ingredients, which have concentrated amounts of flavor and no water, fresh material takes longer to give up its essence.

Dried nuts such as Brazil nuts, hazelnuts, or almonds create an interesting focal point if you're going to pair them with chocolate liqueurs when you serve them. Spices like whole peppercorns, chilies (*see chili infusion instructions on page 154*), dried fennel seed, cinnamon sticks, coffee beans, cocoa beans, vanilla beans, or fresh herbs like rosemary or peppermint also work well solo or in combinations. Use the same measurements we applied to sun-dried berries. Infuse these elements for about one to two weeks. Taste-test your mixture after that time and steep for another week if you want a stronger taste.

There are a few don'ts we'd like to add before you run off to the test lab:

SUN-DRIED CRANBERRY INFUSED VODKA

1 pint grain vodka

1 cup sun-dried cranberries

Transfer vodka into a large canning jar. (Save the bottle.) Add sun-dried cranberries. Seal the container and throw it in the fridge for overnight. Taste-test the mixture. (If it's too light, leave it in the fridge for one more day.) Decant the liquid through a gold-mesh coffee filter back into its original bottle and throw it into the freezer.

SUN-DRIED CHERRY INFUSED VODKA

1 pint grain vodka

1 cup sun-dried cherries

3 large orange twists

Transfer vodka into a large canning jar. (Save the bottle.) Add sun-dried cherries and orange twists. Seal the container and throw it in the fridge for overnight. Taste-test the mixture. (If it's too light, leave it in the fridge for one more day.) Decant the liquid through a gold-mesh coffee filter back into its original bottle and throw it into the freezer.

- Never experiment with more than a pint of a new formula. You don't want to waste good liquor.

- Always use a clean, sterilized, sealable glass container. Never reuse the same jar without cleaning it. Bad kitchen habits invite unwanted flavors.

- Never allow your mixture to infuse in a warm place. You'll change the delicate chemistry that takes place so well in the cool confines of your refrigerator.

- Never drink an infusion that's been left unopened in a warm room for hours. Throw it out.

- Never drink a fresh fruit or herb infusion that's more than one month old. The flavor turns bad very quickly.

Practiced carefully, the alchemy of infusion can result in a surprising array of tastes that will impress both avant-martini sippers and stolid classicists. Who knows, you might go down in the Popular Chemists' Hall of Fame with your genius!

SELECTED BIBLIOGRAPHY

Amis, Kingsley. *On Drink*. (New York: Harcourt Brace Jovanovich, Inc., 1970 and 1972).

Asbury, Herbert (ed.), and Jerry Thomas. *The Bon Vivant's Companion*. (New York: Alfred A. Knopf, 1928).

Blom, Eric (ed.). *Grove's Dictionary of Music and Musicians*, vol. V. (London: Macmillan & Co. Ltd., 1954).

Bredenbek, Magnus. *What Shall We Drink?* (New York: Carlyle House, 1934).

Browne, Charles. *The Gun Club Drink Book*. (New York: Charles Scribner's Sons, 1939).

Coward, Noël. *Autobiography*. (London: Methuen Ltd., 1986).

Doxat, John. *Stirred Not Shaken: The Dry Martini*. (London: Hutchinson Benham Ltd., 1976).

——. *The Book of Drinking*. (London: Tribune Books, 1973).

Edwards, Bill. *How to Mix Drinks*. (Philadelphia: David McKay Company, 1936).

Feery, William C. *Wet Drinks for Dry People*. (New York: William C. Ferry, 1932).

Fleming, Ian. *Casino Royale*. (London: Glidrose Productions Ltd., 1952).

——. *Thrilling Cities*. (London: Glidrose Productions Ltd., 1964).

——. *You Only Live Twice*. (London: Glidrose Productions Ltd., 1964).

Flexner, Stuart Berg. *Listening to America: An Illustrated History of Words and Phrases from Our Lively and Splendid Past*. (New York: Simon & Schuster, 1982).

Gaige, Crosby. *The Standard Cocktail Guide: A Manual of Mixed Drinks Written for the American Host*. (New York: M. Barrows & Co., 1944).

Hemingway, Ernest. *A Farewell to Arms*. (New York: Charles Scribner's Sons, 1929).

——. *Islands in the Stream*. (London: William Collins Sons & Co., Ltd., 1970).

Herter, George Leonard and Berthe E. *Bull Cook and Authentic Historical Recipes and Practices*. (Waseca, MN: Herter's, 1963).

Johnson, Harry. *New and Improved, Illustrated Bartender's Manual or How to Mix Drinks of the Present Style*. (New York: Harry Johnson, 1882).

Lycett, Andrew. *Ian Fleming*. (London: Weidenfeld & Nicholson, 1995).

Mailer, Norman. *Harlot's Ghost*. (New York: Harcourt Brace Jovanovich, 1991).

Mariani, John. *America Eats Out: An Illustrated History of Restaurants, Taverns, Coffee Shops, Speakeasies, and Other Establishments That Have Fed Us for 350 Years*. (New York: William Morrow & Co., Inc., 1991).

Mario, Thomas. *Playboy's Host & Bar Book*. (Chicago: Playboy Press, 1971).

Marx, Harpo, and Rowland Barber. *Harpo Speaks!* (New York: Limelight Editions, 1985).

Mason, Dexter. *The Art of Drinking or What to Make with What You Have*. (New York: Farrar & Rinehart, 1930).

Mencken, H.L. *The American Language: An Inquiry into the Development of English in the United States, 4th ed.* (New York: Alfred A. Knopf, 1963).

Oscar of the Waldorf, *101 Famous Cocktails*. (New York: Kenilworth Press, 1934).

Smith, Mario Cruz. *Polar Star*. (New York: Ballantine Books, 1989).

Thomas, Jerry. *The Bar-Tender's Guide and The Bon Vivant's Companion*. (New York: Dick & Fitzgerald Publishers, 1862).

Watney, John. *Mother's Ruin: A History of Gin*. (London: Peter Owen, Ltd., 1976).

White, Francesca. *Cheers! A Spirited Guide to Liquors and Liqueurs*. (London: Paddington Press, 1977).

Wiley, James E. *The Art of Mixing*. (Philadelphia: Macrae Smith Co., 1932).

Wodehouse, P.G. *Mulliner's Nights*. (London: H. Jenkins, 1966).

INDEX

LAST CALL

When Bill passed away, he was surprised to find himself facing the Pearly Gates. "I always thought Martini drinkers went the other direction," he remarked to St. Peter.

"Who'd you think invented the Martini? Professor Jerry Thomas? It is truly a Divine Inspiration," St. Pete chuckled, leading the newcomer off on a heavenly cook's tour.

Soon they entered the biggest room Bill had ever seen: The walls were covered from floor to ceiling with clocks. "These are the Life Clocks," the Saint pointed out. "They measure every aspect of life performed by every living thing. For instance, every time you ate breakfast, the second hand on your Life Clock ticked."

"And these," Peter remarked when they passed the Cocktail Clocks, "mark every time you've had a cocktail, or even thought about it."

"Where's mine?" Bill asked. They looked all around, but couldn't find it. So St. Peter wandered off to ask one of the attending angels.

"It seems yours is upstairs," Pete said when he returned. "Somebody was using it as a fan."

Martini mixology is a subject that's near and dear to the hearts of authors Anistatia R Miller and Jared M. Brown. After all, Miller grew up on Chicago's Near North Side between cocktail-culture landmarks like the original Playboy Club and the Drake Hotel, while Brown earned his degree in Food & Hotel Management at New York University. They translated their potable passion into their first Web site which they launched on Halloween night in 1995. Since then, "Shaken Not Stirred" (http://www.martinis.com/key/) has garnered awards from McKinley Review, Point Communications, Web Review, and Top 10 percent of Internet Cooking Sites; and it's become a co-branded segment of iVillage's *Vices & Virtues* at America OnLine (keyword: V&V) and on the Web (http://www.vicesandvirtues.com).

When they're not talking about, mixing up, or sipping down Martinis in Manhattan, Vancouver, Chicago, or somewhere out in the woods, they work as contributing editors for *Adobe*'s on-line magazine.